Sauces
dips and salsas

The Confident Cooking Promise of Success

Welcome to the world of Confident Cooking,
where recipes are double-tested by our team
of home economists to achieve a high standard
of success—and delicious results every time.

bay books

C O N T E

Creamy mushroom sauce, page 27

Cucumber and ginger salsa, page 97

White bean, chick pea and herb dip, page 79

Tomato pasta sauce, page 14

Barbecue sauce, page 26

Tzatziki, page 64

The Publisher thanks the following for their assistance: Sunbeam Corporation Ltd; Kambrook; Rice, Surry Hills; Mosmania, Mosman; Camargue, Mosman; Generosity, Mosman; Ruby Star Traders, Pyrmont; Kitchen Kapers, Crows Nest; Shack Homewares, Mosman; The Bay Tree, Woollahra; Orson & Blake, Woollahra. All in NSW. Inside front cover: Béarnaise sauce, page 36

All recipes are double-tested by our team of home economists. When we test our recipes, we rate them for ease of preparation. The following cookery ratings are on the recipes in this book, making them easy to use and understand.

A single Cooking with Confidence symbol indicates a recipe that is simple and generally quick to make —perfect for beginners.

Two symbols indicate the need for just a little more care and a little more time.

Three symbols indicate special dishes that need more investment in time, care and patience—but the results are worth it.

IMPORTANT
Those who might be at risk from the effects of salmonella food poisoning (the elderly, pregnant women, young children and those suffering from immune deficiency diseases) should consult their doctor with any concerns about eating raw eggs.

Zabaglione, page 52

Satay sauce, page 11

Sauces

GREEN PEPPERCORN SAUCE

Shown here with pan-fried steak. Also good with pan-fried chicken breasts.

Preparation time: 10 minutes
Total cooking time: 15 minutes
Serves 4

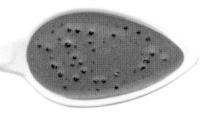

4 steaks or chicken breast
  fillets
1 cup (250 ml/8 fl oz) beef or
  chicken stock
1 cup (250 ml/8 fl oz) cream
2–3 teaspoons canned green
  peppercorns, rinsed and
  drained
1 tablespoon brandy

1 Pan-fry the steak or chicken in a little oil or butter. Remove from the pan, cover with foil and keep warm.
2 Add the stock to the meat juices in the pan. Stir over low heat until boiling, then add the cream and peppercorns. Boil for 8–10 minutes, stirring constantly until slightly thickened. Add the brandy and boil for 1 minute. Serve with the meat.

NUTRITION PER SERVE
Protein 40 g; Fat 30 g; Carbohydrate 2 g; Dietary Fibre 0 g; Cholesterol 165 mg; 1806 kJ (431 cal)

Rinse the peppercorns under running water and set aside.

Pan-fry the meat, then add the stock to the meat juices in the pan.

Boil until reduced slightly, then add the brandy and boil for another minute.

VELOUTE SAUCE

Shown here with grilled chicken. Also good with seafood or veal.

Preparation time: 5 minutes
Total cooking time: 10 minutes
Serves 4

30 g (1 oz) butter
3 tablespoons plain flour
1¹/₂ cups (375 ml/12 fl oz)
**   chicken, fish or veal stock**
lemon juice, to taste
1 tablespoon cream

1 Melt the butter in a pan, add the flour and cook over medium heat for 2 minutes, or until a thick paste has formed—be careful not to brown the mixture or it will colour your sauce.
2 Whisk in the stock a little at a time to prevent the mixture becoming lumpy. Cook the sauce, whisking continuously, for 3–5 minutes—it should be quite thick and not have a floury taste.
3 Season with salt, pepper and lemon juice, adding a little at a time. Finally, stir in the cream. Serve immediately, as this sauce will quickly thicken if left to stand. If necessary, add a little extra stock to thin it down.

NUTRITION PER SERVE
Protein 1 g; Fat 8 g; Carbohydrate 7 g; Dietary Fibre 0 g; Cholesterol 26 mg; 459 kJ (110 cal)

Melt the butter in a pan and cook the flour until it bubbles and thickens.

Whisk in the stock a little at a time to prevent lumps forming.

Add the lemon juice a little at a time, tasting after each addition.

CUMBERLAND SAUCE

Shown here with sliced leg ham. This is a traditional English sauce, usually served cold with ham, turkey, venison or game meats.

Preparation time: 20 minutes
Total cooking time: 20 minutes
Serves 8

2 oranges
1 lemon
225 g (7 oz) redcurrant jelly
2 teaspoons Dijon mustard
2 tablespoons red wine vinegar
1 cup (250 ml/8 fl oz) port

1 Remove the orange and lemon rind with a zester. Place the rind in a small pan with 1 cup (250 ml/8 fl oz) water and bring to the boil. Cook for 5 minutes, then strain the liquid, keeping the rind.
2 Squeeze the juice from the oranges and lemon and place in a pan. Add the jelly, mustard, vinegar, port and reserved rind. Slowly bring to the boil, stirring as the jelly melts. Reduce the heat to simmer gently for 15 minutes. Season to taste and serve at room temperature or cover with plastic wrap and refrigerate for up to a week.

NUTRITION PER SERVE
Protein 1 g; Fat 0 g; Carbohydrate 13 g; Dietary Fibre 2 g; Cholesterol 0 mg; 371 kJ (89 cal)

If you don't have a zester, use a small knife to remove the rind from the fruit.

Place the orange and lemon juice in a pan and add the remaining ingredients.

Bring slowly to the boil, stirring as the redcurrant jelly melts.

HOLLANDAISE

Shown here with asparagus. Good with poached salmon or chicken, egg dishes and steamed or boiled vegetables.

Preparation time: 10 minutes
Total cooking time: 10 minutes
Serves 4

175 g (6 oz) butter
4 egg yolks
1 tablespoon lemon juice or
    white wine vinegar

1 Melt the butter in a small pan. Skim any froth from the surface and discard. Leave the butter to cool.
2 Mix the yolks with 2 tablespoons of water in a small pan. Beat with a wire whisk for about 30 seconds, or until the mixture is pale and foamy. Place over very low heat and whisk for 2–3 minutes, or until thick and the whisk leaves a trail—do not let the pan get too hot or you will have scrambled eggs. Remove from the heat.
3 Add the cooled butter, a little at a time, whisking well between each addition. Try to avoid using the milky butter whey in the bottom of the pan. Stir in the lemon juice or vinegar, season to taste and serve immediately.

NUTRITION PER SERVE
Protein 3 g; Fat 40 g; Carbohydrate 0 g; Dietary Fibre 0 g; Cholesterol 290 mg; 1563 kJ (373 cal)

COOK'S FILE

Food processor method: Place the yolks, water and lemon juice in a food processor and blend for 10 seconds. With the motor running, add the cooled, melted butter in a thin stream.
Microwave method: Melt the butter on High (100%) for 1 minute. Beat the yolks, water and lemon juice together in a bowl and whisk in the butter. Cook for 1 minute 20 seconds on Medium (50%), whisking every 20 seconds. Season to taste.

Melt the butter over gentle heat and skim the froth from the surface.

Put the egg yolks and 2 tablespoons of water in a pan and whisk together.

Whisk until the egg yolk mixture is pale and foamy, then place over the heat.

Add the cooled, melted butter gradually, whisking after each addition.

CHILLI SPICED MANGO SAUCE

Shown here with chargrilled tuna. Also good with chicken, or another strong-flavoured fish such as swordfish.

Preparation time: 35 minutes
Total cooking time: 20 minutes
Serves 4

1 large ripe mango
1 tablespoon oil
1 red onion, finely sliced
3 cloves garlic, finely chopped
4 cm (1¹/2 inch) piece fresh
   ginger, finely chopped
2–3 red chillies, seeded and
   finely chopped
1 tablespoon honey
¹/4 teaspoon ground cinnamon
pinch of ground cardamom
pinch of ground nutmeg
pinch of ground cloves
¹/4 cup (60 ml/2 fl oz) dark rum
¹/4 cup (60 ml/2 fl oz) lime juice
¹/4 cup (7 g/¹/4 oz) coriander
   leaves, chopped

1 Peel the mango and dice the flesh. Heat the oil in a frying pan and add the onion, garlic, ginger and chilli. Cook for about 3–4 minutes, or until the onion is soft.
2 Add the mango, honey, cinnamon, cardamom, nutmeg and cloves. Mix well and bring to the boil. Simmer gently for 5 minutes. Add the rum and simmer for a further 5 minutes. Add the lime juice, coriander and salt and pepper to taste.

NUTRITION PER SERVE
Protein 2 g; Fat 5 g; Carbohydrate 19 g; Dietary Fibre 3 g; Cholesterol 0 mg; 660 kJ (158 cal)

Peel the mango and cut the flesh into small cubes.

Fry the onion, garlic, ginger and chilli until the onion is soft.

Add the rum to the simmering mixture and cook for a further 5 minutes.

Stir the onion, carrot and celery over the heat until softened.

As you brown the mince, break up any lumps with a fork.

Once the mince is browned, add the stock, tomatoes, wine and sugar.

Simmer the sauce for 2 hours, stirring it occasionally. Season to taste.

BOLOGNESE SAUCE

Shown here with spaghetti, but can be served over any hot pasta. Also good as a sauce for pizza bases.

Preparation time: 15 minutes
Total cooking time: 2 hours 15 minutes
Serves 6

**2 tablespoons olive oil
1 large onion, chopped
1 carrot, chopped
1 celery stick, chopped
2 cloves garlic, crushed**

**500 g (1 lb) beef mince
1 cup (250 ml/8 fl oz) beef stock
2 x 425 g (14 oz) cans chopped tomatoes
1 1/2 cups (375 ml/12 fl oz) red wine
1 teaspoon sugar**

1 Heat the olive oil in a large heavy-based pan. Add the onion, carrot and celery and cook, stirring, over medium heat for 5 minutes, or until softened. Add the garlic and cook for 1 minute.
2 Add the mince and cook until well browned. Add the stock, tomatoes, wine and sugar.
3 Bring to the boil, reduce the heat to low and simmer for 2 hours, stirring occasionally. Season to taste with salt and pepper. Serve hot or keep, covered, for up to two days in the refrigerator. Can also be frozen for up to two months.

NUTRITION PER SERVE
Protein 20 g; Fat 10 g; Carbohydrate 5 g; Dietary Fibre 2 g; Cholesterol 53 mg; 923 kJ (221 cal)

SWEET AND SOUR SAUCE

Shown here with spring rolls. Also good with pan-fried, grilled or deep-fried fish and pan-fried pork or lamb.

Preparation time: 10 minutes
Total cooking time: 10 minutes
Serves 6–8

2 tablespoons dry sherry
1 cup (250 ml/8 fl oz) pineapple juice
3 tablespoons white wine vinegar
2 teaspoons soy sauce
2 tablespoons soft brown sugar
2 tablespoons tomato sauce
1 small red capsicum, finely diced
1 tablespoon cornflour

1 Mix together the sherry, pineapple juice, vinegar, soy sauce, brown sugar and tomato sauce in a pan. Cook, stirring constantly, over low heat until the sugar has dissolved. Bring to the boil and add the capsicum.
2 Mix the cornflour in 1 tablespoon water. Add to the pan and cook, stirring, until the mixture boils and thickens. Reduce the heat and simmer for 2 minutes. Serve at once.

NUTRITION PER SERVE (8)
Protein 1 g; Fat 0 g; Carbohydrate 9 g; Dietary Fibre 0 g; Cholesterol 0 mg; 186 kJ (44 cal)

Remove the seeds and membrane from the capsicum before dicing the flesh.

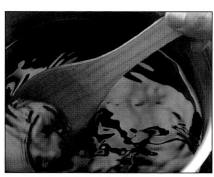

Stir the mixture continuously over low heat until the sugar has dissolved.

Dissolve the cornflour in water so that it doesn't form lumps when added.

SATAY SAUCE

Shown here with chicken skewers. Good with meat or fish skewers, or Gado Gado.

Preparation time: 10 minutes
Total cooking time: 15 minutes
Serves 8

1 tablespoon oil
1 large onion, finely chopped
2 cloves garlic, finely chopped
2 red chillies, finely chopped
1 teaspoon shrimp paste
250 g (8 oz) peanut butter
1 cup (250 ml/8 fl oz) coconut
   milk
2 teaspoons kecap manis or
   thick soy sauce
1 tablespoon tomato sauce

1 Heat the oil in a pan and cook the onion and garlic for 8 minutes over low heat, stirring regularly. Add the chilli and shrimp paste, cook for 1 minute and remove from the heat.
2 Add the peanut butter, return to the heat and stir in the coconut milk and 1 cup (250 ml/8 fl oz) water. Bring to the boil over low heat, stirring so that it does not stick. Add the kecap manis and tomato sauce and simmer for 1 minute. Cool.

NUTRITION PER SERVE
Protein 9 g; Fat 25 g; Carbohydrate 6 g; Dietary Fibre 4 g; Cholesterol 0 mg; 1148 kJ (274 cal)

Chop the chillies very finely. If you prefer a milder taste, remove the seeds first.

Cook the onion and garlic over low heat, then add the chilli and shrimp paste.

Bring to the boil, stirring, then add the kecap manis and tomato sauce.

GAZPACHO SAUCE

Shown here with grilled white fish, but also delicious with chicken, red meat, sausages and steamed asparagus.

Preparation time: 45 minutes
  + 30 minutes refrigeration
Total cooking time: Nil
Serves 8–10

425 g (14 oz) can tomatoes, drained and finely chopped
1 Lebanese cucumber, halved, seeded and finely chopped
1 small red capsicum, finely chopped
1 small green capsicum, finely chopped
1/2 small onion, grated
2 cloves garlic, finely chopped
1/2 cup (40 g/1 1/4 oz) fresh breadcrumbs
2 tablespoons olive oil
2 tablespoons red wine vinegar
1 teaspoon sugar
1/4 teaspoon each of salt and freshly ground black pepper

1 Mix together all the ingredients in a large bowl. Cover and refrigerate for 30 minutes to allow the flavours to develop.

NUTRITION PER SERVE (10)
Protein 2 g; Fat 4 g; Carbohydrate 6 g; Dietary Fibre 1 g; Cholesterol 0 mg; 285 kJ (68 cal)

Halve the cucumber, scrape out the seeds with a spoon and chop the flesh.

Cut the onion in half and grate against the coarse side of a metal grater.

Put all the ingredients in a large bowl and stir to combine.

SORREL AND LEMON SAUCE

Shown here with grilled salmon. Good with chicken and most types of fish.

Preparation time: 25 minutes
Total cooking time: 10 minutes
Serves 4

30 g (1 oz) sorrel leaves, stems
   removed
3 egg yolks
150 g (5 oz) butter, melted
3 tablespoons lemon juice

1 Put the sorrel in a bowl, cover with boiling water and leave for 30 seconds. Drain and refresh in cold water to keep the colour, then chop finely or tear into very small pieces.
2 Put the egg yolks in a bowl and place over a pan of simmering water. Whisk the yolks for about 1 minute, or until they thicken.
3 Continue whisking and gradually drizzle the melted butter into the yolks, a little at a time, whisking after each addition, until the sauce is thick and creamy. Remove the bowl from the heat. Whisk in the lemon juice and the sorrel and season to taste with salt and white pepper.

NUTRITION PER SERVE
Protein 2 g; Fat 34 g; Carbohydrate 1 g;
Dietary Fibre 0 g; Cholesterol 230 mg;
1327 kJ (317 cal)

Place the sorrel leaves in a bowl, cover with boiling water then drain and refresh.

Whisk the yolks in a bowl over a pan of gently simmering water.

Remove the bowl from the heat before adding the lemon juice and sorrel.

TOMATO PASTA SAUCE

Shown here with hot pasta, but also good with pan-fried steaks or veal schnitzel. Can also be used as a sauce for pizza bases.

Preparation time: 25 minutes
Total cooking time: 25 minutes
Serves 4

1.5 kg (3 lb) ripe tomatoes
1 tablespoon olive oil
1 onion, finely chopped
2 cloves garlic, crushed
2 tablespoons tomato paste
1 teaspoon dried oregano
1 teaspoon sugar

1 Score a cross on the base of each tomato, place in a bowl of boiling water for 10 seconds, then plunge into cold water and peel away the skin from the cross. Finely chop the flesh.
2 Heat the oil in a pan. Add the onion and cook, stirring, over medium heat for 3 minutes, or until soft. Add the garlic and cook for 1 minute. Add the tomato, tomato paste, oregano and sugar. Bring to the boil, then reduce the heat and simmer for 20 minutes, or until the sauce has thickened slightly. Season to taste.

NUTRITION PER SERVE
Protein 5 g; Fat 5 g; Carbohydrate 10 g;
Dietary Fibre 6 g; Cholesterol 0 mg;
460 kJ (110 cal)

When the tomatoes are placed in the cold water the skins should peel away easily.

Cook the onion over medium heat for about 3 minutes, then add the garlic.

Add the tomato, tomato paste, dried oregano and sugar.

QUICK AND EASY CRANBERRY SAUCE

Shown here with roast turkey breast. Also good with roast chicken or pork.

Preparation time: 10 minutes
Total cooking time: 5 minutes
Serve 4–6

250 g (8 oz) whole cranberry sauce
1 teaspoon grated orange rind
3 tablespoons orange juice
1 teaspoon ground ginger
1/2 teaspoon ground cardamom
1/4 teaspoon ground allspice

1 Mix together the cranberry sauce, grated orange rind and juice, ginger, cardamom and allspice in a small pan.
2 Bring the cranberry mixture to the boil over medium heat, stirring occasionally. Reduce the heat and leave to simmer for 2 minutes. Allow the sauce to cool to room temperature before serving.

NUTRITION PER SERVE (6)
Protein 0 g; Fat 0 g; Carbohydrate 2 g; Dietary Fibre 0 g; Cholesterol 0 mg; 1335 kJ (320 cal)

Grate the orange using the fine side of a metal grater.

Put the cranberry sauce, orange rind and juice in a pan with the spices.

Bring the mixture to the boil over medium heat, stirring occasionally.

CLASSIC WHITE SAUCE (BECHAMEL)

Shown here with steamed cauliflower and broccoli. Also good with fish or corned beef.

Preparation time: 15 minutes
Total cooking time: 10 minutes
Serves 2–4

1 cup (250 ml/8 fl oz) milk
slice of onion
1 bay leaf
6 peppercorns
30 g (1 oz) butter
1 tablespoon plain flour

1 Put the milk, onion, bay leaf and peppercorns in a small pan. Bring to the boil, remove from the heat and leave to infuse for 10 minutes. Strain the milk, discarding the flavourings.
2 Melt the butter in a small pan and stir in the flour. Cook, stirring, for 1 minute until the mixture is golden and bubbling. Remove from the heat and gradually add the milk, stirring until completely smooth. Return to the heat and stir until the mixture boils. Continue cooking for 1 minute or until thick, remove from the heat and season with salt and white pepper.

NUTRITION PER SERVE (4)
Protein 3 g; Fat 9 g; Carbohydrate 5 g;
Dietary Fibre 0 g; Cholesterol 28 mg;
448 kJ (107 cal)

To add flavour to the milk, infuse with the onion, bay leaf and peppercorns.

Cook the flour and butter, stirring all the time, until golden and bubbling.

Return the pan to the heat and continue stirring to remove any lumps.

CHEESE SAUCE (MORNAY)

Shown here with grilled lobster (lobster mornay). Also good with grilled oysters, steamed or poached fish or vegetables. Mornay sauce is often poured over the top of dishes and then grilled or baked.

Preparation time: 15 minutes
Total cooking time: 10 minutes
Serves 4

1¹/₃ cups (350 ml/11 fl oz) milk
slice of onion
1 bay leaf
6 peppercorns
30 g (1 oz) butter
1 tablespoon plain flour
¹/₂ cup (60 g/2 oz) finely grated
   Cheddar
¹/₄ teaspoon mustard powder

1 Put the milk, onion, bay leaf and peppercorns in a small pan. Bring to the boil, remove from the heat and leave to infuse for 10 minutes. Strain the milk, discarding the flavourings.
2 Melt the butter in a small pan and add the flour. Cook, stirring, for 1 minute until the mixture is golden and bubbling. Add the infused milk, a little at a time, stirring between each addition until completely smooth. Continue stirring until the mixture boils and thickens. Boil for 1 minute more and then remove from the heat.

Add the cheese and mustard and stir until the cheese has melted and the sauce is smooth. Season to taste with salt and pepper.

NUTRITION PER SERVE
Protein 7 g; Fat 15 g; Carbohydrate 4 g; Dietary Fibre 0 g; Cholesterol 50 mg; 730 kJ (174 cal)

Once the milk has been left to infuse for 10 minutes, strain it.

Add the infused milk very gradually, stirring to prevent lumps forming.

Add the cheese and mustard powder and stir until the cheese has melted.

CHUNKY ROASTED RED ONION SAUCE

Shown here with grilled steak and mashed potatoes. This sauce is also great with barbecued meats.

Preparation time: 20 minutes
Total cooking time: 1 hour 20 minutes
Serves 6–8

500 g (1 lb) red onions, thinly
    sliced
1 kg (2 lb) pickling onions
3 large cloves garlic
2 tablespoons olive oil
1.5 kg (3 lb) Roma tomatoes
1 teaspoon salt
1/4 cup (7 g/1/4 oz) chopped
    oregano
440g (14 oz) can Italian peeled
    tomatoes
1 tablespoon muscatel liqueur or
    brandy
1 tablespoon soft brown sugar

1 Preheat the oven to moderately hot 200°C (400°F/Gas 6) Place the red onion, pickling onions and garlic cloves in a large roasting tin with half the olive oil. Roll the onions in the oil so that they are lightly coated.

2 Halve the tomatoes lengthways and add to the tin. Drizzle with the remaining olive oil, salt and oregano and roast for 1 hour.

3 Use a pair of kitchen scissors to roughly cut up the canned tomatoes, while they are still in the tin. Spoon the chopped tomatoes and their juice into the roasting tin, taking care not to break up the roasted tomatoes. Drizzle the muscatel or brandy over the top and sprinkle with the brown sugar. Return to the oven and roast for a further 20 minutes. Serve hot.

NUTRITION PER SERVE (8)
Protein 5 g; Fat 5 g; Carbohydrate 13 g; Dietary Fibre 5 g; Cholesterol 0 mg; 528 kJ (126 cal)

Red onions will give a lovely colour to the sauce. Peel them and slice thinly.

Add the tomatoes to the roasting tin and sprinkle with oil, salt and oregano.

Use scissors to chop up tinned tomatoes without losing the juice.

Drizzle the muscatel or brandy over the pan and sprinkle with soft brown sugar.

DEMI-GLACE

Shown here with beef tournedos, but good with any type of beef steak.

Preparation time: 50 minutes
Total cooking time: 6 hours
Serves 8

Beef Stock
1 kg (2 lb) beef bones
1 tablespoon oil
1 onion, chopped
2 carrots, chopped
5 parsley stalks
2 bay leaves
6 peppercorns

Espagnole
2 tablespoons oil
2 carrots, finely chopped
1 onion, finely chopped
1 stalk celery, finely chopped
1 tablespoon flour
1/2 teaspoon tomato paste
bouquet garni

1 To make the beef stock, preheat the oven to hot 220°C (440°F/Gas 7). Roast the bones for 1 hour, or until browned. Heat the oil in a large pan and brown the vegetables, being careful not to burn them. Add the bones, parsley, bay leaves and peppercorns and cover with cold water. Bring to the boil, reduce the heat and simmer for 3–4 hours, skimming off the fat as it rises to the surface. Add a little more cold water if needed. You should have about 3 1/2 cups (875 ml/28 fl oz) of stock—if you have more, continue reducing; if less, add a little water. Strain and cool. Remove any fat which sets on the surface.

2 To make the espagnole, heat the oil in a pan and brown the vegetables. Add the flour and cook, stirring, until browned. Add 2 1/2 cups (600 ml/20 fl oz) of the beef stock with the tomato paste and bouquet garni and bring to the boil. Reduce the heat, half-cover the pan and simmer, skimming off any fat, for 30 minutes, or until reduced to 1 cup (250 ml/8 fl oz). Sieve and leave to cool.

3 To make the demi-glace, put the espagnole and the remaining cup of stock in a pan and simmer until reduced by half. Strain thoroughly through a fine mesh sieve or muslin.

NUTRITION PER SERVE
Protein 130 g; Fat 8 g; Carbohydrate 5 g; Dietary Fibre 2 g; Cholesterol 2 mg; 400 kJ (97 cal)

COOK'S FILE

Note: Don't use ready-made stock—it is far too salty for this recipe.
Variation: To make a beef glace, reduce the strained stock to a thick sticky liquid which will set to a jelly when cold. This gives a rich flavour when added to sauces.

To make the espagnole, heat the oil in a pan and brown the chopped vegetables.

Half-cover the pan and leave to simmer for 30 minutes, skimming off any fat.

Strain the sauce again through a fine sieve or muslin.

SKORDALIA (GREEK GARLIC SAUCE)

Shown with fried eggplant (lightly coat the eggplant with flour before frying). Traditionally served with steamed beetroot and beetroot greens, or fish croquettes, but served today with seafood, steak, lamb or chicken.

Preparation time: 35 minutes
Total cooking time: 15 minutes
Serves 6

2 large floury potatoes (about
   500 g/1 lb in total), chopped
5 cloves garlic, crushed
60 g (2 oz) ground almonds
2/3 cup (170 ml/5¹/2 fl oz) olive
   oil
2 tablespoons white wine
   vinegar

1 Boil the potatoes until tender, drain then mash. Mash the garlic and almonds into the potato.
2 Add the oil gradually, mashing until smooth. Add the vinegar and season to taste. Mash well, adding a tablespoon of water at a time (you will need 3–4) to give a thick creamy consistency. Serve cold. Can be kept, covered, in the fridge for up to 1 day.

NUTRITION PER SERVE
Protein 4 g; Fat 33 g; Carbohydrate 10 g; Dietary Fibre 3 g; Cholesterol 0 mg; 1472 kJ (352 cal)

Mash the garlic and almonds into the mashed potato.

Pour in the oil gradually, mashing until the mixture is thick and smooth.

Add the water a tablespoon at a time. You will need three to four tablespoons.

PESTO

Shown here with pasta. Also good with grilled fish, chicken or tomatoes. Pesto can even be used as a spread on crackers and is ideal for finger food.

Preparation time: 15 minutes
Total cooking time: 3 minutes
Serves 6

1/3 cup (50 g/1³/4 oz) pine nuts
250 g (8 oz) basil leaves
2 cloves garlic, crushed
1/3 cup (35 g/1¹/4 oz) finely
    grated Parmesan
1/3 cup (80 ml/2³/4 fl oz) olive oil

1 Cook the pine nuts in a dry frying pan for 2–3 minutes, or until lightly browned. Place in a food processor with the basil, garlic and Parmesan and process until finely chopped.

2 With the motor running, add the oil in a thin stream. Season if necessary.

NUTRITION PER SERVE
Protein 3 g; Fat 20 g; Carbohydrate 0 g; Dietary Fibre 1 g; Cholesterol 6 mg; 820 kJ (196 cal)

COOK'S FILE

Variations: Pesto is so popular at present that you will find restaurants offering all manner of variations—sun-dried tomato or capsicum pestos are popular. For a slightly peppery taste, use fresh rocket or watercress instead of basil. Try macadamia nuts or pistachios to replace the pine nuts (you don't need to toast them first).

Toast the pine nuts in a dry frying pan until they are golden brown.

Put the basil, garlic, Parmesan and pine nuts in a food processor.

Add the olive oil in a thin stream with the motor running.

Mayonnaise and dressings

Mayonnaise is something that most of us expect to buy in a jar in the supermarket and take a chance as to whether it's rich and creamy or, as if often the case, rather gluey and oversweet. Try making your own—it's actually very easy and you'll get a good-quality result every time.

MAYONNAISE

Whisk together 2 egg yolks, 1 teaspoon Dijon mustard and 1 tablespoon lemon juice for 30 seconds, or until light and creamy. Add 3/4 cup (185 ml/6 fl oz) olive oil, about a teaspoon at a time, whisking continuously. You can add the oil more quickly as the mayonnaise thickens. Season, to taste, with salt and white pepper.

Aternatively, place the egg yolks, mustard and lemon juice in a food processor and mix for 10 seconds. With the motor running, add the oil in a slow, thin stream. Season, to taste. Makes about 1 cup (250 ml/8 fl oz).

NUTRITION PER TABLESPOON
Protein 0 g; Fat 15 g; Carbohydrate 0 g; Dietary Fibre 0 g; Cholesterol 30 mg; 581 kJ (139 cal)

AIOLI (GARLIC MAYONNAISE)

Mix together 1 cup (250 ml/8 fl oz) mayonnaise with 3 crushed cloves of garlic. Season, to taste, with salt and pepper. Makes about 1 cup (250 ml/8 fl oz).

NUTRITION PER TABLESPOON
Protein 0 g; Fat 15 g; Carbohydrate 0 g; Dietary Fibre 0 g; Cholesterol 30 mg; 584 kJ (139 cal)

THOUSAND ISLAND DRESSING

Mix together 11/2 cups (375 ml/12 fl oz) mayonnaise, 1 tablespoon sweet chilli sauce, 1–2 tablespoons tomato sauce, 1/4 red capsicum and 1/4 green capsicum, finely chopped, 1 tablespoon chopped chives and 1/2 teaspoon sweet paprika. Stir well and season. Cover and refrigerate for up to 3 days. Thousand Island Dressing is traditionally served on lettuce leaves. Makes 12/3 cups (410 ml/13 fl oz).

NUTRITION PER TABLESPOON
Protein 1 g; Fat 15 g; Carbohydrate 1 g; Dietary Fibre 0 g; Cholesterol 32 mg; 647 kJ (154 cal)

GREEN GODDESS DRESSING

Mix together 11/2 cups (375 ml/12 fl oz) mayonnaise, 4 mashed anchovy fillets, 4 finely chopped spring onions, 1 crushed clove garlic, 1/4 cup (7 g/1/4 oz) chopped flat-leaf parsley, 1/4 cup (15 g/1/2 oz) finely chopped chives and 1 teaspoon tarragon vinegar. Serve as a salad dressing or with seafood. Makes about 12/3 cups (410 ml/13 fl oz).

NUTRITION PER TABLESPOON
Protein 1 g; Fat 15 g; Carbohydrate 0 g; Dietary Fibre 0 g; Cholesterol 32 mg; 632 kJ (151 cal)

BLUE CHEESE DRESSING

Mix together ¹/₂ cup (125 ml/4 fl oz) mayonnaise, ¹/₄ cup (60 ml/2 fl oz) thick cream, 1 teaspoon white wine vinegar and 1 tablespoon finely chopped chives. Crumble 50 g (1³/₄ oz) blue cheese into the mixture and gently stir through. Season with salt and white pepper. Can be kept refrigerated, covered, for up to 2 days. Serve over asparagus, boiled new potatoes, jacket potatoes or with a green salad. Makes about 1 cup (250 ml/8 fl oz).

NUTRITION PER TABLESPOON
Protein 1 g; Fat 15 g; Carbohydrate 0 g; Dietary Fibre 0 g; Cholesterol 36 mg; 656 kJ (157 cal)

CAESAR SALAD DRESSING

Cook an egg in boiling water for 1 minute. Break the egg into a small bowl and add 2 tablespoons white wine or tarragon vinegar, 2 teaspoons Dijon mustard, 2 chopped anchovy fillets and 1 crushed clove garlic. Mix together with a small wire whisk. Add ¹/₂ cup (125 ml/4 fl oz) oil in a thin stream, whisking continuously until the mixture is smooth and creamy. Keep, covered, in the fridge for up to 2 days. Serve on Caesar salad (cos lettuce, bacon, croutons and Parmesan). Makes about ³/₄ cup (185 ml/6 fl oz).

NUTRITION PER TABLESPOON
Protein 1 g; Fat 14 g; Carbohydrate 0 g; Dietary Fibre 0 g; Cholesterol 23 mg; 532 kJ (127 cal)

TARTARE SAUCE

Mix together 1¹/₂ cups (375 ml/12 fl oz) mayonnaise, 1 tablespoon finely chopped onion, 1 teaspoon lemon juice, 1 tablespoon chopped gherkins, 1 teaspoon chopped capers, ¹/₄ teaspoon Dijon mustard and 1 tablespoon finely chopped parsley. Mix well and season with salt and pepper. Top with a few capers to serve. Makes about 1²/₃ cups (410 ml/13 fl oz).

NUTRITION PER TABLESPOON
Protein 0 g; Fat 15 g; Carbohydrate 0 g; Dietary Fibre 0 g; Cholesterol 32 mg; 627 kJ (150 cal)

COCKTAIL SAUCE

Mix together 1 cup (250 ml/8 fl oz) mayonnaise, 3 tablespoons tomato sauce, 2 teaspoons Worcestershire sauce, ¹/₂ teaspoon lemon juice and 1 drop of Tabasco sauce. Season with salt and pepper. Keep, covered, in the fridge for up to 2 days. Makes about 1¹/₄ cups (315 ml/10 fl oz).

NUTRITION PER TABLESPOON
Protein 0 g; Fat 15 g; Carbohydrate 1 g; Dietary Fibre 0 g; Cholesterol 30 mg; 608 kJ (145 cal)

Top, from left: Mayonnaise; Thousand Island; Blue Cheese; Tartare Sauce.
Bottom, from left: Aioli; Green Goddess; Caesar Salad; Cocktail Sauce.

ROASTED RED CAPSICUM SAUCE

Shown here with grilled chicken, but good with any grilled meats or vegetables. Also try with grilled Haloumi cheese or egg dishes, such as soufflés.

Preparation time: 30 minutes
Total cooking time: 1 hour 15 minutes
Serves 8

2 red capsicums
2 tablespoons olive oil
1 red onion, roughly chopped
1–2 cloves garlic, crushed
425 g (14 oz) can chopped
   tomatoes
1/2 cup (30 g/1 oz) chopped
   parsley
1/2 cup (30 g/1 oz) chopped basil
   leaves
1 tablespoon tomato paste
1 tablespoon caster sugar

1 Cut the capsicums into quarters, remove the membrane and seeds and grill, skin-side-up, until blackened. Cool in a plastic bag for 10 minutes, peel away the skin and chop roughly.
2 Heat the oil in a pan and cook the onion and garlic for 2 minutes, or until soft but not brown. Add the tomatoes, parsley, basil, tomato paste, sugar and 1 1/2 cups (375 ml/12 fl oz) water.
3 Add the chopped capsicum and cook, stirring often, over very low heat for 45 minutes to 1 hour, or until thick. Leave to cool slightly, then purée in batches in a food processor. Season with salt and black pepper.

NUTRITION PER SERVE
Protein 2 g; Fat 5 g; Carbohydrate 9 g; Dietary Fibre 2 g; Cholesterol 0 mg; 370 kJ (90 cal)

Once the skin is blackened it should peel away easily.

Cook the onion and garlic until they are softened but not browned.

Add the chopped capsicum to the sauce and cook for up to 1 hour, or until thick.

APPLE SAUCE

Shown here with pan-fried pork fillet, but also good with roast pork or chops.

Preparation time: 20 minutes
Total cooking time: 10 minutes
Serves 6–8

4 green apples, cored, peeled
  and chopped
2 teaspoons caster sugar
2 cloves
1 cinnamon stick
1–2 teaspoons lemon
  juice

1 Put the apple, sugar, cloves, cinnamon and 1/2 cup (125 ml/4 fl oz) water in a small pan, cover and simmer over low heat for 10 minutes, or until the apple is soft. Remove the cloves and cinnamon. Mash the apples (or press through a sieve for a finer sauce). Stir in the lemon juice, to taste.

NUTRITION PER SERVE (8)
Protein 0 g; Fat 0 g; Carbohydrate 12 g; Dietary Fibre 2 g; Cholesterol 0 mg; 202 kJ (48 cal)

Try to cut the apples into even-sized pieces so they cook at the same rate.

Remove the cloves and cinnamon from the apple.

Mash the cooked apple or press through a sieve if you prefer a finer sauce.

BARBECUE SAUCE

Shown here with a hamburger. Great with just about any barbecued meat— chops, steak or sausages.

Preparation time: 15 minutes
Total cooking time: 10 minutes
Serves 4

2 teaspoons oil
1 small onion, finely chopped
1 tablespoon malt vinegar
1 tablespoon soft brown sugar
1/3 cup (80 ml/2³/4 fl oz) tomato
  sauce
1 tablespoon Worcestershire
  sauce

1 Heat the oil in a small pan and cook the onion over low heat for 3 minutes, or until soft, stirring occasionally.
2 Add the remaining ingredients and bring to the boil. Reduce the heat and simmer for 3 minutes, stirring occasionally. Serve warm or at room temperature. Can be kept, covered and refrigerated, for up to a week.

NUTRITION PER SERVE
Protein 1 g; Fat 10 g; Carbohydrate 17 g; Dietary Fibre 1 g; Cholesterol 0 mg; 648 kJ (155 cal)

Chop the onion very finely so the sauce has a smooth texture.

Cook the onion over low heat, stirring occasionally, until soft.

Add the remaining ingredients to the pan and bring to the boil.

CREAMY MUSHROOM SAUCE

Shown here with pan-fried chicken breasts. Also good with beef or veal steaks.

Preparation time: 10 minutes
Total cooking time: 15 minutes
Serves 4

4 chicken breasts or steaks
30 g (1 oz) butter
350 g (11 oz) small button mushrooms, sliced
2 tablespoons white wine
1/2 cup (125 ml/4 fl oz) chicken stock
1/2 cup (125 ml/4 fl oz) cream
1 clove garlic, crushed
1 tablespoon chopped chives

1 Pan-fry the chicken or meat in a little oil or butter. Remove from the pan, cover with foil and keep warm. Add the butter and mushrooms to the pan juices and stir over medium heat for 5 minutes, or until soft and golden.
2 Add the wine, stock, cream and garlic, and bring to the boil. Cook for 5 minutes, stirring constantly, until the sauce thickens slightly. Stir in the chives and serve immediately.

NUTRITION PER SERVE
Protein 37 g; Fat 23 g; Carbohydrate 1 g; Dietary Fibre 0 g; Cholesterol 142 mg; 1541 kJ (368 cal)

Chop the chives into short, even lengths with a sharp knife.

Add the butter and sliced mushrooms to the pan juices and cook until golden.

Add the wine, stock, cream and garlic, and bring to the boil.

GRAVY

Shown here with roast beef. Great with lamb, chicken or pork and, of course, roast potatoes and Yorkshire pudding.

Preparation time: 5 minutes
Total cooking time: 10 minutes
Serves 8

pan juices from the roast
2 tablespoons plain flour
2 cups (500 ml/16 fl oz) beef or
  chicken stock

1 After removing the roast and covering it lightly with foil to keep it warm, pour off any excess fat from the tin. Sprinkle the flour over the pan juices and stir well, scraping any bits from the bottom of the roasting tin. Transfer the roasting tin to the stove top and cook, stirring, over medium heat for 1–2 minutes.

2 Add the stock a little at a time, stirring well. Make sure the stock and the flour mixture are well combined before you add more stock, or you will have lumpy gravy. Bring the gravy to the boil and stir over the heat for 1 minute, or until the gravy has thickened a little. Season to taste and serve immediately with the meat.

NUTRITION PER SERVE
Protein 0 g; Fat 5 g; Carbohydrate 2 g;
Dietary Fibre 0 g; Cholesterol 7 mg;
238 kJ (57 cal)

Sprinkle the flour over the pan juices, stirring well to scrape up any bits.

Add the stock a little at a time, stirring constantly to prevent lumps forming.

Let the gravy boil for about 1 minute, or until it thickens to your taste.

BLUE CHEESE, PECAN AND COGNAC GRILLING SAUCE

Shown here spread over pear halves and grilled until melted. Also great on bread, burgers, oysters and avocado.

Preparation time: 15 minutes
Total cooking time: 2 minutes
Serves 8

100 g (3½ oz) pecans
75 g (2½ oz) softened butter
200 g (6½ oz) Gorgonzola cheese
1 tablespoon chopped parsley
2 tablespoons Cognac

1 Spread the pecans on a tray and toast under the grill for 1–2 minutes, or until they start to change colour. Cool for 5 minutes, then roughly chop.

2 Mix together the butter and cheese with a fork. Stir in the pecans and parsley and add the Cognac. Season with pepper and mix well. Spread over cooked food, bread or fruit and grill until melted and bubbling.

NUTRITION PER SERVE
Protein 6 g; Fat 25 g; Carbohydrate 1 g; Dietary Fibre 1 g; Cholesterol 50 mg; 1038 kJ (248 cal)

COOK'S FILE

Note: Best made a couple of days in advance, to let the flavours develop. Can be kept, covered and refrigerated, for up to 5 days.

Toast the pecans under the grill, then chop roughly.

Mash the butter and cheese with a fork until they are well blended.

Add the Cognac and mix together well with the fork.

MINT AND YOGHURT SAUCE

Shown here with tandoori chicken. Good with any Indian food, especially curries, but also delicious with many seafood dishes (try with chargrilled baby octopus).

Preparation time: 20 minutes
Total cooking time: Nil
Serves 10

1 red onion, roughly chopped
1 green chilli, seeded and
    roughly chopped
3 cm (1¹/4 inch) piece fresh
    ginger, peeled and chopped
¹/2 cup (15 g/¹/2 oz) firmly
    packed coriander leaves
1¹/4 cups (25 g/³/4 oz) firmly
    packed mint leaves
2 tablespoons fish sauce
3 teaspoons caster sugar
500 g (1 lb) plain thick yoghurt

1 Place the onion, chilli, ginger, coriander, mint, fish sauce and sugar in a food processer and purée until smooth. Fold through the yoghurt just before serving.

NUTRITION PER SERVE
Protein 3 g; Fat 2 g; Carbohydrate 5 g; Dietary Fibre 0 g; Cholesterol 8 mg; 203 kJ (48 cal)

COOK'S FILE

Note: It is actually the membrane of the chilli which holds its fieriness. When you have removed the seeds and membrane, be careful to scrub your hands with hot soapy water to prevent skin irritation.

Remove the seeds and membrane from the chilli before chopping.

Purée the sauce in a food processor or blender.

Fold the yoghurt into the puréed sauce just before serving.

JAPANESE SOY, MIRIN AND SESAME SAUCE

Shown here with chargrilled scallops. Also good with noodle and vegetable dishes, beef salad or pan-fried steak.

Preparation time: 15 minutes
Total cooking time: Nil
Serves 6

1/2 cup (125 ml/4 fl oz) tahini
2–3 cloves garlic, crushed
1 cup (30 g/1 oz) coriander
  leaves
1/3 cup (80 ml/2 3/4 fl oz) rice
  vinegar
3 tablespoons lime juice
2 tablespoons Japanese soy
  sauce
2 tablespoons mirin
3 tablespoons oil
1 tablespoon sesame oil

1 Place the tahini and garlic in a food processor and process briefly. Add the coriander, rice vinegar, lime juice, soy sauce and mirin. Process until smooth.
2 Mix the oil and sesame oil together and, with the motor still running, slowly add to the food processor. The sauce will thicken but still have a pourable consistency.

NUTRITION PER SERVE
Protein 5 g; Fat 15 g; Carbohydrate 1 g; Dietary Fibre 3 g; Cholesterol 0 mg; 690 kJ (165 cal)

Put the tahini and garlic in a food processor and process briefly.

Add the coriander, rice vinegar, lime juice, soy sauce and mirin.

Add the combined oils slowly, with the motor running continuously.

31

ROASTED WALNUT SAUCE

Shown here with pasta, but also good with grilled vegetables. The sauce can also be thinned down with extra olive oil and served as a salad dressing.

Preparation time: 15 minutes
Total cooking time: 5 minutes
Serves 8–10

300 g (10 oz) walnut pieces
1 tablespoon extra virgin olive oil
1/4 teaspoon paprika
pinch of salt
2 slices white bread, crusts removed
300 ml (10 fl oz) milk
1 clove garlic, crushed
1/3 cup (20 g/3/4 oz) coarsely chopped parsley
1/2 cup (125 ml/4 fl oz) light olive oil
3 tablespoons grated Parmesan

1 Preheat the oven to moderately hot 190°C (375°F/Gas 5). Put the walnuts on a baking tray, toss with the extra virgin olive oil, then sprinkle with the paprika and salt and toss well to ensure the nuts are well coated. Roast for 5 minutes, then allow to cool.
2 Put the bread in a bowl, pour over the milk and leave to soak until soft.
3 Put the walnuts, bread and milk mixture, garlic and parsley in a food processor and mix until very fine and with an even consistency. With the motor running, slowly pour in the olive oil until the sauce becomes thick. Add the Parmesan, season to taste and process briefly to blend before serving. The sauce is very rich and can be kept in an airtight container in the fridge for up to three days.

NUTRITION PER SERVE (10)
Protein 7 g; Fat 37 g; Carbohydrate 5 g; Dietary Fibre 2 g; Cholesterol 7 mg; 1565 kJ (374 cal)

The parsley need only be coarsely chopped as it will be processed later.

Sprinkle the paprika and salt over the walnuts and toss to coat them well.

Remove the crusts from the bread and leave to soak with the milk.

Add the olive oil to the food processor with the motor running.

PAWPAW SAUCE

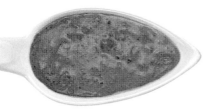

Shown here with grilled pork loin. Also good with pan-fried pork and beef, lamb, chicken and turkey.

Preparation time: 35 minutes
+ 20 minutes standing
Total cooking time: Nil
Serves 4

250 g (8 oz) ripe pawpaw or
  papaya
3 tablespoons cream
1 tablespoon dry white wine
2 teaspoons wholegrain mustard
2 spring onions, finely chopped

1 Cut the pawpaw or papaya in half, discarding the seeds and peel. Chop the flesh finely and place in a bowl with all of the juices from the fruit.

2 Add the cream, wine, mustard and spring onion to the pawpaw. Season to taste with salt and pepper and whisk well. Cover and leave to stand for 20 minutes before serving.

NUTRITION PER SERVE
Protein 1 g; Fat 7 g; Carbohydrate 5 g; Dietary Fibre 2 g; Cholesterol 20 mg; 348 kJ (83 cal)

COOK'S FILE

Note: Slightly overripe fruit will give more flavour and juice.

Remove the tough outer leaves and chop the spring onion very finely.

Cut the pawpaw in half, scoop out the seeds and discard the peel.

Whisk the sauce together, then leave for the flavours to develop before serving.

Vinaigrettes

Vinaigrettes are classic salad dressings made from a combination of oil and vinegar. Many of us have been dressing our salad greens with a plain vinaigrette since we discovered balsamic vinegar and extra virgin olive oil, but there are other variations along this wonderful theme. The following recipes will give you ideas for herbs, fruit and even pistachios in your dressing.

BASIC VINAIGRETTE

Put 2 tablespoons white wine vinegar, $1/3$ cup (80 ml/$2^3/4$ fl oz) light olive oil and 1 teaspoon Dijon mustard in a small screw-top jar. Season with salt and cracked black pepper and shake until well blended. Will keep, covered, in the fridge for up to 2 days. Makes $1/3$ cup (80 ml/$2^3/4$ fl oz).

NUTRITION PER TABLESPOON
Protein 0 g; Fat 19 g; Carbohydrate 0 g; Dietary Fibre 0 g; Cholesterol 0 mg; 710 kJ (170 cal)

LEMON THYME AND LIME VINAIGRETTE

Put $2/3$ cup (170 ml/$5^1/2$ fl oz) light olive oil, $1/3$ cup (80 ml/ $2^3/4$ fl oz) lime juice, 2 tablespoons lemon thyme leaves and 1 teaspoon honey in a screw-top jar. Season with salt and pepper and shake well. Will keep, covered, in the refrigerator for up to 2 days. Makes 1 cup (250 ml/8 fl oz).

NUTRITION PER TABLESPOON
Protein 0 g; Fat 13 g; Carbohydrate 1 g; Dietary Fibre 0 g; Cholesterol 0 mg; 509 kJ (122 cal)

STRAWBERRY VINAIGRETTE

Place $1/3$ cup (80 ml/$2^3/4$ fl oz) light olive oil, 2 tablespoons strawberry vinegar, $1/2$ teaspoon Dijon mustard and $1/2$ teaspoon sugar in a screw-top jar. Season with salt and pepper and shake well. Will keep, covered, in the fridge for up to 2 days. Makes $1/2$ cup (125 ml/4 fl oz).

NUTRITION PER TABLESPOON
Protein 0 g; Fat 13 g; Carbohydrate 0 g; Dietary Fibre 0 g; Cholesterol 0 mg; 478 kJ (114 cal)

BALSAMIC AND BASIL VINAIGRETTE

Put 2 tablespoons balsamic vinegar, $1/3$ cup (80 ml/$2^3/4$ fl oz) extra virgin olive oil, 1 crushed clove garlic and 2 tablespoons shredded basil in a screw-top jar. Season, to taste, and shake until mixed. Refrigerate, covered, for up to 2 days. Makes $1/3$ cup (80 ml/$2^3/4$ fl oz).

NUTRITION PER TABLESPOON
Protein 0 g; Fat 19 g; Carbohydrate 0 g; Dietary Fibre 0 g; Cholesterol 0 mg; 712 kJ (170 cal)

LEMON GRASS
AND LIME VINAIGRETTE

Mix 1/2 cup (125 ml/4 fl oz) oil, 1/2 cup (125 ml/4 fl oz) lime juice, 3 teaspoons sesame oil, 2 tablespoons finely sliced lemon grass, 1 crushed clove garlic and 2 teaspoons soft brown sugar in a screw-top jar. Season with salt and pepper and shake well to combine. Will keep, covered, in the refrigerator for up to 2 days. Makes 1 1/4 cups (315 ml/10 fl oz).

NUTRITION PER TABLESPOON
Protein 0 g; Fat 9 g; Carbohydrate 0 g; Dietary Fibre 0 g; Cholesterol 0 mg; 340 kJ (80 cal)

PISTACHIO AND
TARRAGON VINAIGRETTE

Put 1/3 cup (80 ml/2 3/4 fl oz) light olive oil, 1 tablespoon pistachio oil, 2 tablespoons white wine vinegar, 1 tablespoon chopped pistachios, 1 tablespoon chopped tarragon and 1/4 teaspoon sugar in a screw-top jar. Season with salt and pepper and shake well to combine. Will keep, covered, in the refrigerator for up to 2 days. Makes 1/3 cup (80 ml/2 3/4 fl oz).

NUTRITION PER TABLESPOON
Protein 0 g; Fat 24 g; Carbohydrate 1 g; Dietary Fibre 0 g; Cholesterol 0 mg; 887 kJ (212 cal)

ORANGE AND MUSTARD
SEED VINAIGRETTE

Mix 1/3 cup (80 ml/2 3/4 fl oz) orange juice, 2 tablespoons vinegar, 1/3 cup (80 ml/2 3/4 fl oz) light olive oil, 1/2 teaspoon finely grated orange rind and 2 teaspoons wholegrain mustard in a screw-top jar. Season with salt and pepper and shake well. Will keep, covered, in the fridge for up to 2 days. Makes 2/3 cup (160 ml/5 1/2 fl oz).

NUTRITION PER TABLESPOON
Protein 0 g; Fat 13 g; Carbohydrate 0 g; Dietary Fibre 0 g; Cholesterol 0 mg; 478 kJ (114 cal)

RASPBERRY VINAIGRETTE

Place 1/3 cup (80 ml/2 3/4 fl oz) hazelnut oil, 2 tablespoons raspberry vinegar, 5 finely chopped raspberries and 1/2 teaspoon sugar in a small screw-top jar. Season with salt and white pepper and shake to blend. Will keep, covered, in the fridge for up to 2 days. Makes 1/3 cup (80 ml/2 3/4 fl oz).

NUTRITION PER TABLESPOON
Protein 0 g; Fat 19 g; Carbohydrate 1 g; Dietary Fibre 1 g; Cholesterol 0 mg; 733 kJ (175 cal)

Top, from left: Basic Vinaigrette; Strawberry; Lemon Grass and Lime; Orange and Mustard Seed. Bottom, from left: Lemon Thyme and Lime; Balsamic and Basil; Pistachio and Tarragon; Raspberry.

BEARNAISE SAUCE

Shown with pan-fried steak. Good with roast beef or lamb, or poached salmon.

Preparation time: 10 minutes
Total cooking time: 15 minutes
Serves 4

¹/₃ cup (80 ml/2³/₄ fl oz) white
  wine vinegar
2 spring onions, roughly
  chopped
2 teaspoons chopped tarragon
2 egg yolks
125 g (4 oz) butter, cubed

1 Put the white wine vinegar, spring onion and tarragon in a small pan. Bring to the boil, then reduce the heat slightly and simmer until the mixture has reduced by a third. Allow to cool completely and then strain the vinegar into a heatproof bowl.
2 Add the egg yolks to the bowl, then place the bowl over a pan of barely simmering water. Whisk until the mixture is thick and pale. Add the butter, a cube at a time, whisking between each addition until the mixture is thick and smooth. Season to taste with salt and pepper and serve immediately.

NUTRITION PER SERVE
Protein 2 g; Fat 28 g; Carbohydrate 1 g; Dietary Fibre 0 g; Cholesterol 169 mg; 1085 kJ (259 cal)

Boil the vinegar with the onions and tarragon to give flavour, then strain.

Place the bowl over a pan of simmering water so the mixture doesn't overheat.

Add the butter a cube at a time, whisking well after each addition.

Remove the seeds and membrane from the capsicum and cut into pieces.

Put the roasted capsicum and the whole peeled garlic cloves in the food processor.

ALMOND AND RED CAPSICUM SAUCE

Shown here with lamb cutlets cut from a rack. Good with steak, chicken or seafood, in particular tuna and prawns.

Preparation time: 15 minutes
Total cooking time: 20 minutes
Serves 6

1 large red capsicum
2 cloves garlic, unpeeled
125 g (4 oz) flaked almonds
4 tablespoons red wine vinegar
  (see note)
2/3 cup (170 ml/5^1/$_2$ fl oz) olive
  oil
2 tablespoons finely chopped
  parsley

1 Cut the capsicum into large pieces, removing the seeds and membrane. Place, skin-side-up, under a hot grill for 10 minutes, then add the garlic. When the skin of the capsicum blackens and blisters, remove it and the garlic from the grill and cool in a plastic bag. Peel the capsicum and garlic and transfer to a food processor.
2 Reduce the temperature of the grill to moderate. Spread the almonds on a baking tray and toast under the grill, stirring once or twice, until lightly golden. Set aside to cool for 5 minutes, then add to the capsicum and garlic in the food processor.
3 Process until smooth then, with the motor running, slowly add the red wine vinegar. Season to taste with salt and freshly ground black pepper. With the motor running, gradually pour in the oil, then add 3 tablespoons boiling water. The consistency should be the thickness of mayonnaise. Add the parsley and process briefly.

NUTRITION PER SERVE
Protein 5 g; Fat 38 g; Carbohydrate 3 g; Dietary Fibre 3 g; Cholesterol 0 mg; 1556 kJ (372 cal)

Lightly toast the almonds under the grill, then add to the processor.

At the end of processing, add the boiling water to thin down the sauce.

COOK'S FILE

Note: Best made a day in advance. If you are making on the day of serving, use 3 tablespoons of red wine vinegar.

SOUR CHERRY SAUCE

Shown here with roast duck. Good with turkey, pork, ham, smoked chicken and any type of poultry or game.

Preparation time: 10 minutes
Total cooking time: 10 minutes
Serves 6

680 g (1 lb 6 oz) jar pitted
    morello (sour) cherries
1/3 cup (80 ml/2³/4 fl oz) port
1 teaspoon Dijon mustard
1/2 teaspoon grated orange
    rind
3 tablespoons orange juice,
    strained
1 chicken stock cube
1 tablespoon cornflour

1 Drain the cherries, reserving 1 cup (250 ml/8 fl oz) of the liquid. Place the liquid in a pan with the port, mustard, orange rind and juice. Crumble in the stock cube and bring to the boil.
2 Blend the cornflour with a couple of tablespoons of water and stir into the sauce. Bring to the boil, add the cherries, reduce the heat and simmer for 5 minutes, stirring occasionally. Season to taste and then serve hot.

NUTRITION PER SERVE
Protein 1 g; Fat 0 g; Carbohydrate 24 g; Dietary Fibre 2 g; Cholesterol 0 mg; 469 kJ (112 cal)

Drain the jar of morello cherries, reserving a cup of the liquid.

Crumble the stock cube into the liquid and then bring to the boil.

Dissolve the cornflour in a little water before adding, or it will form lumps.

SPICED COCONUT SAUCE

Shown here with white fish fillets. Also good with baked whole fish or pan-fried lamb, steamed or stir-fried Asian greens or over lettuce as a salad dressing.

Preparation time: 30 minutes
Total cooking time: 5 minutes
Serves 2–4

40 g (1¼ oz) bunch coriander (roots, stems and leaves)
2 teaspoons oil
3 cm (1¼ inch) fresh ginger, peeled and grated
2 stalks lemon grass (white part only), finely chopped
2 small red chillies, finely chopped
1 clove garlic, finely chopped
3 tablespoons coconut cream, plus extra if necessary
2 tablespoons rice vinegar
1 teaspoon soft brown sugar

1 Finely chop the coriander, keeping the roots, stems and leaves separate. Heat the oil in a frying pan over low heat and cook the ginger, lemon grass, chilli, coriander root and garlic, stirring constantly, for 3 minutes, or until aromatic. Add the coconut cream, stirring well. Increase the heat to high and bring the sauce to a rapid boil. Cook for about 1 minute until the mixture looks oily (this is the coconut cream separating or 'cracking'). Do not let the sauce burn. Add another 2 tablespoons of coconut cream if the sauce becomes too thick.

2 Transfer to a bowl and add the coriander stem and leaves, rice vinegar and sugar. Stir well and add salt and more sugar, to taste. Serve at room temperature.

NUTRITION PER SERVE (4)
Protein 1 g; Fat 6 g; Carbohydrate 3 g; Dietary Fibre 1 g; Cholesterol 0 mg; 270 kJ (65 cal)

Chop the bunch of coriander, keeping the root separate from the leaves and stem.

Cook the ginger, lemon grass, chilli, garlic and coriander root until aromatic.

Transfer to a bowl and add the coriander, rice vinegar and sugar.

BLACK BEAN SAUCE

Shown here with grilled chicken. Also good with prawns, crab, stir-fried beef, pork or lamb and chargrilled salmon.

Preparation time: 10 minutes
Total cooking time: 15 minutes
Serves 6

2 tablespoons salted black
  beans
1 tablespoon oil
1 small onion, finely chopped
1 tablespoon finely chopped
  fresh ginger
1 clove garlic, finely chopped
1 red chilli, seeded and finely
  chopped
1¼ cups (315 ml/10 fl oz)
  chicken stock
2 teaspoons cornflour
2 teaspoons sesame oil

1 Rinse the black beans under cold water for 3–4 minutes to remove any excess saltiness. Drain well.
2 Heat the oil in a small pan and add the onion, ginger, garlic and chilli. Cook over low heat until the onion is soft but not browned. Add the chicken stock and bring to the boil. Reduce the heat and simmer for 5 minutes.
3 Mix the cornflour and 1 tablespoon of water in a small bowl and add to the pan. Keep stirring and the mixture will thicken. Allow to simmer for

3 minutes, then add the beans and sesame oil and mix together well.

NUTRITION PER SERVE
Protein 1 g; Fat 1 g; Carbohydrate 2 g; Dietary Fibre 0 g; Cholesterol 0 mg; 76 kJ (18 cal)

COOK'S FILE

Note: Black beans are available canned or in vacuum packs from Asian food stores. Don't confuse them with Mexican black turtle beans from health food shops.

Rinse the black beans under running water to get rid of excess saltiness.

Cook until the onion is soft but not browned, then add the stock.

Simmer the sauce for 3 minutes, then stir in the beans and sesame oil.

CHINESE LEMON SAUCE

Shown here with deep-fried dim sims. Also good with spring rolls and dumplings, vegetables, chicken and fish.

Preparation time: 15 minutes
Total cooking time: 10 minutes
Serves 4

3 tablespoons lemon juice
3 tablespoons chicken stock
1 tablespoon honey
1 tablespoon sugar
1/2 teaspoon grated fresh
    ginger
1 tablespoon cornflour
2 spring onions, sliced on the
    diagonal

1 Put the lemon juice, stock, honey, sugar and ginger in a pan with 1/2 cup (125 ml/4 fl oz) water. Stir over medium heat until the sugar dissolves.
2 Increase the heat and bring to the boil. Blend the cornflour with a little water and add to the pan, stirring constantly until the sauce boils and thickens. Remove from the heat, stir in the spring onion and season with salt.

NUTRITION PER SERVE
Protein 0 g; Fat 0 g; Carbohydrate 12 g;
Dietary Fibre 0 g; Cholesterol 0 mg;
228 kJ (54 cal)

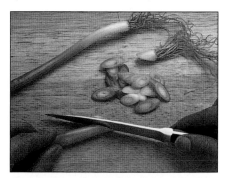

For a more decorative finish, slice the spring onions on the diagonal.

Stir the mixture over the heat until the sugar dissolves.

When the mixture boils, the cooked cornflour will cause it to thicken.

SPICY ROASTED PUMPKIN AND RED CAPSICUM SAUCE

Shown here with pan-fried lamb fillets. Also good with beef, chicken, tuna steaks or jacket potatoes.

Preparation time: 30 minutes
Total cooking time: 1 hour 20 minutes
Serves 4

500 g (1 lb) pumpkin (try Jap, butternut or golden nugget)
2 cloves garlic, crushed
2 tablespoons olive oil
1 red capsicum
2 teaspoons cumin seeds
2 teaspoons coriander seeds
1 cup (250 ml/8 fl oz) vegetable stock

1 Preheat the oven to moderately hot 200°C (400°F/Gas 6). Cut the pumpkin into wedges and place in a baking dish. Combine the garlic and oil and drizzle over the pumpkin. Season well with salt and cracked pepper. Cook for 1 hour, or until the pumpkin is tender. Allow to cool slightly.

2 Cut the capsicum into large flat pieces, removing the membranes and seeds. Place, skin-side-up, under a hot grill for 10 minutes, or until the skin blackens and blisters. Cool under a tea towel or in a plastic bag, peel away the skin and cut the flesh into strips.

3 Put the cumin and coriander seeds in a small frying pan and dry-fry for 5 minutes. Grind in a small food processor or mortar and pestle. Remove the skin from the pumpkin and put the flesh, ground spices and stock in a food processor. Purée the mixture until smooth, then transfer to a pan and heat through gently. Add the capsicum strips and stir through.

NUTRITION PER SERVE
Protein 4 g; Fat 10 g; Carbohydrate 12 g; Dietary Fibre 3 g; Cholesterol 0 mg; 655 kJ (156 cal)

Drizzle the combined garlic and oil over the pumpkin and season well.

Peel the blackened skin away from the capsicum and cut the flesh into strips.

Put the cumin and coriander seeds in a dry frying pan and toast for 5 minutes.

Purée the roast pumpkin, dry-fried spices and stock until smooth.

LIME AND CHILLI SAUCE

Shown here with chargrilled tuna. Also good with smoked, grilled or poached salmon, seafood, chicken, asparagus or artichoke, and as a dip with poppadoms.

Preparation time: 15 minutes
Total cooking time: Nil
Serves 4

1/2 cup (25 g/3/4 oz) chopped and
   firmly packed mint leaves
1/2 cup (25 g/3/4 oz) chopped
   coriander leaves
1 teaspoon grated lime rind
1 tablespoon lime juice
1 teaspoon grated fresh ginger
1 jalapeno chilli, seeded and
   finely chopped
1 cup (250 g/8 oz) plain yoghurt

1 Mix together the mint, coriander, lime rind, lime juice, ginger and chilli. Fold in the yoghurt and season with salt and cracked pepper to taste.

NUTRITION PER SERVE
Protein 3 g; Fat 2 g; Carbohydrate 4 g; Dietary Fibre 1 g; Cholesterol 10 mg; 226 kJ (54 cal)

COOK'S FILE

Note: Jalapeno chillies are smooth and thick-fleshed and are available both red and green. They are quite fiery and you can use a less powerful variety of chilli if you prefer.

It's a good idea to wear gloves to de-seed chillies, to prevent skin irritation.

Mix together the mint, coriander, lime rind, juice, ginger and chilli.

Check the taste of the sauce before seasoning with salt and black pepper.

LEEK AND PINE NUT SAUCE

Shown here with veal cutlets. Also good with grilled or braised steak or lamb, salmon, chicken, or over mashed potato.

Preparation time: 35 minutes
Total cooking time: 20 minutes
Serves 6

2 leeks, about 500 g (1 lb)
1 onion, finely chopped
1¹/2 cups (375 ml/12 fl oz) chicken stock
100 ml (3¹/2 fl oz) dry white wine
6 egg yolks
¹/2 cup (125 ml/4 fl oz) cream
¹/3 cup (50 g/1³/4 oz) pine nuts, toasted and roughly chopped

1 Finely chop the white part of the leeks, put in a pan with the onion, stock and wine and simmer, covered, for 15 minutes, or until very soft.
2 Purée the mixture in a food processor, then pass through a sieve. Return to the pan and whisk in the yolks and cream. Whisk over low heat for 2–3 minutes, or until slightly thickened—take care not to boil or it will curdle. Stir in the pine nuts.

NUTRITION PER SERVE
Protein 6 g; Fat 20 g; Carbohydrate 5 g; Dietary Fibre 3 g; Cholesterol 207 mg; 974 kJ (233 cal)

Wash leeks thoroughly and cut away the tough green leaves before chopping.

Purée the mixture and then pass through a sieve so it is very smooth.

Whisk the sauce over low heat until it has thickened slightly.

MINT SAUCE

Shown here with roast rack of lamb, but delicious with any roast or grilled lamb.

Preparation time: 5 minutes + standing
Total cooking time: 5 minutes
Serves 4

$^1/3$ cup (90 g/3 oz) sugar
2 tablespoons malt vinegar
$^1/3$ cup (20 g/$^3/4$ oz) finely
chopped mint leaves

1 Put the sugar in a pan with 3 tablespoons water. Stir over low heat, without boiling, until dissolved. Bring to the boil, reduce the heat and simmer for 3 minutes without stirring. Remove from the heat.

2 Mix the sugar mixture with the vinegar and mint. Cover and leave for 10 minutes for the flavours to develop, before serving.

NUTRITION PER SERVE
Protein 0 g; Fat 0 g; Carbohydrate 22 g; Dietary Fibre 0 g; Cholesterol 0 mg; 366 kJ (88 cal)

Finely chop the fresh mint leaves with a sharp knife.

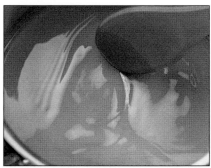

Stir the sugar and water over low heat without letting it boil.

Mix together the sugar mixture, vinegar and mint and allow to stand.

45

ROCKET SALSA VERDE

Shown here with pan-fried fish. Also good with meat and chicken or as a pasta sauce.

Preparation time: 30 minutes
+ 4 hours standing
Total cooking time: Nil
Serves 4

1/3 cup (20 g/3/4 oz) fresh
    breadcrumbs
1/2 cup (125 ml/4 fl oz) olive oil
2 tablespoons lemon juice
1 clove garlic, crushed
4 anchovy fillets, finely chopped
3/4 cup (30 g/1 oz) firmly packed
    rocket leaves, chopped

1/4 cup (5 g/1/4 oz) firmly packed
    flat-leaf parsley, chopped
1 tablespoon capers, chopped

1 Put all the ingredients in a bowl, mix together and season well with freshly ground black pepper.
2 Cover with plastic wrap and leave at room temperature for 4 hours. Stir well just before serving.

NUTRITION PER SERVE
Protein 1 g; Fat 30 g; Carbohydrate 4 g;
Dietary Fibre 0 g; Cholesterol 1 mg;
1200 kJ (287 cal)

It's a good idea to rinse the capers before using to wash off the brine.

Remove any tough stems from the rocket before chopping the leaves.

Mix together all the ingredients in a large bowl then leave at room temperature.

ROASTED CASHEW SATAY SAUCE

Shown here with pork skewers. Also good with chicken satays, barbecued meats, sausages and hamburgers.

Preparation time: 30 minutes
Total cooking time: 20 minutes
Serves 10

250 g (8 oz) roasted cashews
150 g (5 oz) roasted peanuts
1 teaspoon cumin seeds
1 teaspoon coriander seeds
1/4 teaspoon fenugreek seeds
375 ml (12 fl oz) coconut milk
3 teaspoons kecap manis or
    thick soy sauce
2 teaspoons sweet chilli sauce
1 teaspoon soft brown sugar

1 Preheat the oven to warm 160°C (315°F/Gas 2–3). Spread the cashews and peanuts on a baking tray, being careful not to overcrowd them. Roast for 10 minutes, then allow to cool.
2 Finely grind the cumin, coriander and fenugreek seeds with a mortar and pestle. Put in a small pan and dry-fry over low heat for about 3 minutes, shaking the pan regularly, until the spices are very aromatic.
3 Put the nuts and spices in a food processor and finely chop. Add the remaining ingredients and salt and pepper and process until a soft chunky sauce. If you prefer a thin sauce, add 2–3 tablespoons of water.
4 Transfer to a small pan and heat gently for 5 minutes, until warm.

NUTRITION PER SERVE
Protein 9 g; Fat 28 g; Carbohydrate 10 g; Dietary Fibre 2 g; Cholesterol 0 mg; 1382 kJ (330 cal)

Spread the cashews and peanuts on a baking tray and roast in the oven.

Grind the cumin, coriander and fenugreek seeds with a mortar and pestle.

Finely grind the nuts and spices in a food processor, then add the other ingredients.

47

TOMATO AND RED CHILLI SAUCE

Shown here with pan-fried steak. Good with any meat, chicken, vegetables, fish or seafood, such as mussels.

Preparation time: 25 minutes
Total cooking time: 1 hour
Serves 4–6

1 tablespoon olive oil
1 onion, finely chopped
2–3 cloves garlic, crushed
1–2 small red chillies, finely chopped
2 teaspoons grated fresh ginger
1 kg (2 lb) tomatoes, peeled, seeded and chopped
1 cup (180 g/6 oz) lightly packed soft brown sugar
1 cup (30 g/1 oz) basil, chopped
1 cup (250 ml/8 fl oz) red wine vinegar
1/3 cup (80 ml/2³/4 fl oz) dry sherry
1–2 teaspoons sweet chilli sauce

1 Heat the oil in a large pan and cook the onion, garlic, chilli and ginger, stirring, for 2 minutes. Do not allow the mixture to brown.

2 Add the tomato, brown sugar, basil, vinegar, sherry and chilli sauce. Cook over low heat, stirring frequently to prevent burning, for 1 hour or until thick and syrupy.

NUTRITION PER SERVE (6)
Protein 2 g; Fat 3 g; Carbohydrate 35 g; Dietary Fibre 3 g; Cholesterol 0 mg; 812 kJ (194 cal)

COOK'S FILE

Note: Leave out the sweet chilli sauce if you prefer a milder flavour.

Remove the skin from the tomatoes and scoop out the seeds with a teaspoon.

Cook the onion, garlic, chilli and ginger before adding the other ingredients.

Simmer the sauce for 1 hour, stirring often to prevent it sticking and burning.

BREAD SAUCE

Shown here with roasted spatchcock.
Serve warm with roast chicken, turkey,
goose or game meat.

Preparation time: 20 minutes
Total cooking time: 15 minutes
Serves 4

2 cloves
1 onion
1 cup (250 ml/8 fl oz) milk
1 bay leaf
50 g (1¾ oz) fresh breadcrumbs
   (made using about 3 slices of
   day-old bread)
3 tablespoons cream

1 Push the cloves into the onion and
put in a pan with the milk and bay
leaf. Bring to the boil, then remove
from the heat, cover and leave for
10 minutes. Remove the onion and leaf.
2 Add the breadcrumbs to the pan
and season. Return to the heat, cover
and simmer gently for 10 minutes,
stirring occasionally. Stir in the cream.

NUTRITION PER SERVE
Protein 4 g; Fat 8 g; Carbohydrate 12 g;
Dietary Fibre 1 g; Cholesterol 25 mg;
556 kJ (133 cal)

*Stud the onion with the whole cloves to
add flavour to the milk.*

*Once the milk has infused for 10 minutes
lift out the onion and bay leaf.*

*Stir in the fresh breadcrumbs and then
return the pan to the heat.*

49

CHAMPAGNE APPLE SAUCE

Shown here with pan-fried pork chops. Also good with roast pork, a whole roast ham or turkey.

Preparation time: 15 minutes
Total cooking time: 15 minutes
Serves 6–8

3/4 **cup (185 ml/6 fl oz) Champagne or sparkling wine**
4 **green apples, peeled, cored and chopped**
1/2 **teaspoon finely grated lemon rind**
1 **tablespoon finely chopped lemon thyme or thyme**
45 g (1 1/2 oz) **butter, chopped**

1 Place the Champagne in a pan and boil for 1 minute. Add the apple and lemon rind, cover and simmer until the apple is tender. Stir in the lemon thyme and leave to cool for 5 minutes.
2 Transfer the mixture to a food processor and purée. Add the butter gradually, processing between additions. Season the sauce to taste with salt and pepper and serve warm or at room temperature.

NUTRITION PER SERVE (8)
Protein 0 g; Fat 5 g; Carbohydrate 11 g; Dietary Fibre 2 g; Cholesterol 14 mg; 416 kJ (99 cal)

Peel the apples, remove the cores and chop the flesh.

Simmer the apple and lemon rind until the apple is tender. Add the lemon thyme.

Add the butter gradually, processing after each addition.

BEURRE BLANC

Shown here with steamed artichoke hearts. Also good with seafood and steamed or boiled vegetables.

Preparation time: 10 minutes
Total cooking time: 10 minutes
Serves 4

2 French shallots, chopped
3 tablespoons white wine
vinegar
220 g (7 oz) unsalted butter,
cubed
lemon juice, to taste

1 Put the shallots, vinegar and 3 tablespoons water in a pan and bring to the boil. Reduce the heat and simmer until reduced to 2 tablespoons. Remove from the heat, strain into a clean pan and return to low heat.
2 Whisk in the butter a few pieces at a time. The sauce will thicken as the butter is added until it is the same consistency as cream. Season to taste with salt, pepper and lemon juice.

NUTRITION PER SERVE
Protein 1 g; Fat 46 g; Carbohydrate 2 g; Dietary Fibre 0 g; Cholesterol 139 mg; 1755 kJ (419 cal)

COOK'S FILE

Hint: Serve warm: if it is too hot the butter will separate; too cold and it will set. Keep it warm in a bowl over a pan of gently simmering water.
Variations: For a chicken or fish Beurre Blanc, use 4 tablespoons of very strong chicken or fish stock and 1 tablespoon of white wine instead of the white wine vinegar. Reduce to 2 tablespoons, then proceed as above.

For Orange Beurre Blanc, simmer together 120 g (4 oz) of the unsalted butter, 4 tablespoons of white wine and the juice and zest of 2 oranges, until reduced to 3 tablespoons. Whisk in the remaining cubes of butter, then stir in 4 tablespoons of cream.

Chop the French shallots, then simmer in the vinegar and water until reduced.

Strain the reduced mixture into a clean pan, discarding the chopped shallot.

Whisk the butter into the mixture, a few cubes at a time.

ZABAGLIONE

Shown here with fresh blueberries and strawberries. Serve with just about any poached or grilled fruits (pears, nectarines, peaches) or with sponge fingers (langues de chats).

Preparation time: 10 minutes
Total cooking time: 10 minutes
Serves 10–12

8 egg yolks
¹/3 cup (90 g/3 oz) caster sugar
1¹/4 cups (315 ml/10 fl oz)
   Marsala

1 Beat the egg yolks and sugar in a heatproof bowl with electric beaters until pale yellow.
2 Put the bowl over a gently simmering pan of water and beat continuously, adding the Marsala gradually. Beat for 5 minutes, or until thick and frothy. To test if it is ready, dip a metal spoon into the Zabaglione, hold it up and if the mixture slides down the back it is not yet thickened enough. If you can draw a line through the Zabaglione with a spoon and leave a trail, it is ready. Serve immediately or keep refrigerated for up to 1 day and serve chilled.

NUTRITION PER SERVE (12)
Protein 2 g; Fat 3 g; Carbohydrate 11 g; Dietary Fibre 0 g; Cholesterol 119 mg; 426 kJ (102 cal)

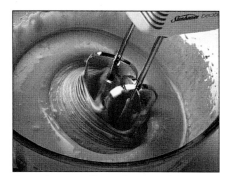

Beat the egg yolks and sugar with electric beaters until pale yellow.

Place the bowl over a pan of simmering water. Add the Marsala as you beat.

When the Zabaglione leaves a trail from a spoon, it is ready to serve.

EASY VANILLA CUSTARD

Shown here with apple pie, but delicious with just about any sweet pie, pastry or pudding you can think of.

Preparation time: 10 minutes
Total cooking time: 10 minutes
Serves 6

1 cup (250 ml/8 fl oz) milk
1/4 cup (60 ml/2 fl oz) cream
3 egg yolks
1/3 cup (90 g/3 oz) caster sugar
2 teaspoons cornflour
1 teaspoon vanilla essence

1 Put the milk and cream in a pan and bring to the boil. Immediately remove the pan from the heat.

2 Whisk the egg yolks together with the sugar and cornflour in a heatproof bowl. Slowly pour the hot milk and cream over the egg mixture, whisking continuously. Return the mixture to the pan and stir over low heat for 5 minutes, or until the custard starts to bubble and thicken—do not allow it to boil, but remove from the heat immediately. Whisk in the vanilla essence and serve.

NUTRITION PER SERVE
Protein 3 g; Fat 8 g; Carbohydrate 18 g; Dietary Fibre 0 g; Cholesterol 108 mg; 647 kJ (155 cal)

Whisk the egg yolks with the sugar and cornflour in a heatproof bowl.

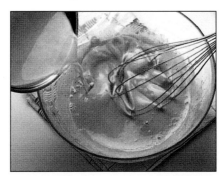

Place the bowl on a tea towel to stop it slipping while you whisk in the hot milk.

Remove the pan from the heat and whisk in the vanilla.

ICED ORANGE SAUCE

Shown here with fresh mango. Also good with fresh berries, grilled figs, peaches or nectarines and waffles.

Preparation time: 15 minutes + freezing
Total cooking time: Nil
Serves 8

1 litre rich vanilla ice cream
3 tablespoons orange juice
   concentrate
1–2 tablespoons Cointreau or
   Grand Marnier

1 Refrigerate the ice cream until slightly softened and put the orange juice concentrate in the freezer until semi-frozen.

2 Transfer the ice cream to a bowl and stir very gently until almost smooth. Stir in the concentrate and liqueur. The sauce should have the consistency of thick cream. Use the sauce immediately, rather than refreezing it.

NUTRITION PER SERVE
Protein 3 g; Fat 9 g; Carbohydrate 16 g;
Dietary Fibre 0 g; Cholesterol 21 mg;
662 kJ (158 cal)

Place the orange juice concentrate in the freezer until it is semi-frozen.

Stir the softened ice cream very gently until it is almost smooth.

Add the orange juice concentrate and Cointreau to the ice cream.

BURNT SUGAR SAUCE

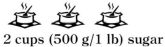

Shown here with waffles and ice cream. Also good with pancakes or crepes, and fresh or poached fruit.

Preparation time: 5 minutes
  + overnight refrigeration
Total cooking time: 20 minutes
Serves 6

2 cups (500 g/1 lb) sugar

1 Mix the sugar and 1 cup (250 ml/ 8 fl oz) water in a deep pan and stir over low heat, without boiling, until the sugar has dissolved. Increase the heat and bring to the boil. Brush down the side of the pan with a pastry brush dipped in water to prevent sugar crystals from forming. Reduce the heat and leave to simmer, without stirring, until the mixture turns dark brown and begins to smell burnt.

2 Place a tea towel in the sink to stand the pan on (the hot pan can cause the sink to buckle if it is not protected). Transfer the pan to the sink, place a tea towel over your arm to protect it and add 3/4 cup (185 ml/ 6 fl oz) water to the pan. The mixture will splutter violently. When the spluttering subsides, return the pan to medium heat and stir with a wooden spoon until the caramel dissolves and comes to the boil. Reduce the heat and simmer for 1 minute.

3 Leave the sauce in the pan to cool, then pour into an airtight container and refrigerate overnight to let the sauce thicken.

NUTRITION PER SERVE
Protein 0 g; Fat 0 g; Carbohydrate 83 g; Dietary Fibre 0 g; Cholesterol 0 mg; 1333 kJ (319 cal)

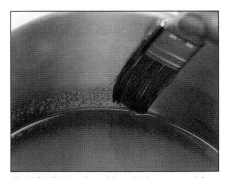

Brush down the side of the pan with a pastry brush to prevent crystals forming.

Place a towel over your arm and take care when adding the water.

Stir with a wooden spoon until the caramel dissolves and comes to the boil.

COCONUT LIME ANGLAISE

Shown here with steamed pudding. Serve warm or cold with poached fruit, fruit pies and tarts, and jelly desserts.

Preparation time: 15 minutes
Total cooking time: 10 minutes
Serves 4

3 egg yolks
3 tablespoons caster sugar
1 teaspoon cornflour
3/4 cup (185 ml/6 fl oz) coconut
   cream
1/2 cup (125 ml/4 fl oz) milk
1/4 cup (60 ml/2 fl oz) cream
1 teaspoon finely grated lime
   rind

1 Chill a bowl or heatproof jug in the refrigerator. Using electric beaters, whisk the egg yolks, caster sugar and cornflour together in a heatproof bowl, until light and creamy. Place the coconut cream, milk, cream and lime rind in a small pan and heat until almost boiling, then pour onto the egg mixture, beating constantly.
2 Return the mixture to the pan and stir over low heat for about 5 minutes, or until slightly thickened—do not boil or the sauce will curdle.
3 Strain into the bowl and serve immediately, or cover the surface with plastic wrap to stop a skin forming.

NUTRITION PER SERVE
Protein 4 g; Fat 14 g; Carbohydrate 10 g; Dietary Fibre 1 g; Cholesterol 135 mg; 770 kJ (185 cal)

COOK'S FILE

Variation: Add a tablespoon of lime juice to the sauce just before straining.

Whisk together the egg yolks, caster sugar and cornflour.

Pour the hot mixture onto the egg mixture, whisking continuously.

Strain the sauce into the chilled bowl or jug and serve immediately, or cover.

PRALINE CREAM SAUCE

Shown here with poached pears but good with any fresh or poached fruit, pancakes, crepes, or chocolate cake.

Preparation time: 15 minutes
Total cooking time: 15 minutes
Serves 6

½ cup (80 g/2¾ oz) blanched
    almonds, toasted
½ cup (125 g/4 oz) caster sugar
⅓ cup (100 g/3½ oz) chocolate
    hazelnut spread
300 ml (10 fl oz) chilled cream

1 To make almond praline, line a baking tray with baking paper and arrange the almonds on it in a single layer. Mix the sugar together with 4 tablespoons of water in a small pan. Stir over low heat, without boiling, until the sugar has dissolved. Without stirring, cook the mixture until it turns golden, then quickly pour it over the almonds. Allow to set until hard, then chop in a food processor until broken down into fine crumbs.

2 Place the hazelnut spread in a heatproof bowl over a pan of hot water until the spread softens slightly. Remove the bowl from the pan and stir in the cream. Whisk the mixture until smooth (do not overbeat or it will become grainy), then fold in the praline crumbs.

NUTRITION PER SERVE
Protein 4 g; Fat 54 g; Carbohydrate 23 g; Dietary Fibre 1 g; Cholesterol 68 mg; 3254 kJ (777 cal)

COOK'S FILE

Note: The praline can be stored in an airtight container for up to a day. Praline is a hard mixture of toffee and nut and can be made using other nuts such as pecans or macadamias.

Place the almonds on a baking tray lined with paper and pour over the syrup.

Soften the hazelnut spread in a bowl over a pan of hot water.

Whisk the mixture until it is smooth, then fold in the praline.

HOT CHOCOLATE SAUCE

Shown here with fruit kebabs. Serve hot over ice cream, profiteroles, waffles, pancakes, poached fruit or puddings.

Preparation time: 10 minutes
Total cooking time: 10 minutes
Serves 8

250 g (8 oz) good-quality dark
    cooking chocolate, chopped
3/4 cup (185 ml/6 fl oz) cream
50 g (1³/4 oz) butter
1 tablespoon golden syrup
2 tablespoons chocolate or
    coffee liqueur, such as
    Baileys, Tia Maria or Kahlua

1 Place the chocolate, cream, butter and syrup in a pan and stir over low heat until the mixture is smooth. Stir in the liqueur and serve hot or cold.

NUTRITION PER SERVE
Protein 2 g; Fat 24 g; Carbohydrate 25 g; Dietary Fibre 0 g; Cholesterol 47 mg; 1360 kJ (325 cal)

COOK'S FILE

Note: Store for up to 1 month in the fridge and reheat gently to serve. Add a little more cream if slightly grainy.

The quality of the chocolate will make all the difference to this sauce.

Put the chocolate, cream, butter and syrup in a pan and heat gently.

Once the sauce is smooth, stir in the liqueur and serve.

BRANDY CREAM SAUCE

Shown here with plum pudding. Also good with chocolate pudding, fresh or poached fruit and fruit pies.

Preparation time: 15 minutes
Total cooking time: Nil
Serves 12

2 eggs, separated
1/3 cup (90 g/3 oz) caster sugar
1/3 cup (80 ml/2³/4 fl oz) brandy
1 cup (250 ml/8 fl oz) cream,
 lightly whipped

1 Beat the egg yolks and sugar until the mixture is thick and creamy and the sugar has dissolved. Stir in the brandy and fold in the cream.

2 Beat the egg whites in a small dry bowl until soft peaks form. Fold into the sauce and serve immediately.

NUTRITION PER SERVE
Protein 1 g; Fat 10 g; Carbohydrate 8 g;
Dietary Fibre 0 g; Cholesterol 58 mg;
528 kJ (126 cal)

COOK'S FILE

Variation: Whisky or Calvados can be used instead of brandy.

Beat together the egg yolks and sugar until thick and creamy.

Lightly fold in the whipped cream, using a metal spoon.

Beat the egg whites and then fold into the sauce, trying to keep the volume.

CREME ANGLAISE

Shown here with fruit tart. Good with all fruit pastries and warmed cakes, and anything you would serve with ordinary custard.

Preparation time: 10 minutes
Total cooking time: 10 minutes
Serves 4

3 egg yolks
2 tablespoons caster sugar
1½ cups (375 ml/12 fl oz) milk
½ teaspoon vanilla essence

1 Whisk the yolks and sugar in a heatproof bowl for 2 minutes, or until light and creamy. Heat the milk in a small pan until almost boiling, then pour onto the mixture, whisking constantly.
2 Return the mixture to the pan and stir over low heat for about 5 minutes, or until slightly thickened, enough to coat the back of a spoon. Do not allow to boil or the custard will curdle. Remove the pan from the heat, stir in the vanilla essence and transfer to a jug. Serve immediately, or lay a piece of plastic wrap directly on the surface of the custard to prevent it forming a skin.

NUTRITION PER SERVE
Protein 5 g; Fat 7 g; Carbohydrate 13 g; Dietary Fibre 0 g; Cholesterol 146 mg; 558 kJ (133 cal)

Whisk together the egg yolks and sugar in a bowl.

Place the bowl on a tea towel to prevent it slipping as you whisk.

Cover the surface of the custard with plastic wrap to stop it forming a skin.

BUTTERSCOTCH SAUCE

Shown with grilled bananas. Also good with grilled peaches, nectarines or other fruit, puddings, waffles and crepes.

Preparation time: 5 minutes
Total cooking time: 15 minutes
Serves 6

125 g (4 oz) butter
1/2 cup (90 g/3 oz) soft brown sugar
2 tablespoons golden syrup
1/2 cup (125 ml/4 fl oz) cream
1 teaspoon vanilla essence

1 Put the butter and sugar in a pan and stir over low heat until the butter has melted and the sugar dissolved.
2 Bring to the boil and add the syrup and cream. Reduce the heat and simmer for 10 minutes, or until slightly thickened. Remove from the heat and add the vanilla essence. Serve hot or cold.

NUTRITION PER SERVE
Protein 1 g; Fat 26 g; Carbohydrate 23 g; Dietary Fibre 0 g; Cholesterol 82 mg; 1343 kJ (321 cal)

Put the butter and sugar in a pan and stir over low heat until dissolved.

Add the syrup and cream to the pan and simmer for 10 minutes.

Remove the sauce from the heat and stir in the vanilla essence.

61

CHOCOLATE RUM SAUCE

Shown here with crepes. Also good with pancakes, waffles, steamed puddings, brownies, ice cream and fruit kebabs.

Preparation time: 10 minutes
Total cooking time: 10 minutes
Serves 8

1 cup (185 g/6 oz) lightly
   packed soft brown sugar
60 g (2 oz) butter
¾ cup (185 ml/6 fl oz) cream
1 tablespoon dark rum
60 g (2 oz) dark chocolate,
   chopped

1 Put the sugar, butter and cream in a pan and bring to the boil over gentle heat, stirring. Reduce the heat and simmer for 4 minutes.
2 Remove from the heat and add the rum and chocolate. Stir until the chocolate has melted. Cool to room temperature before serving, to allow the sauce to thicken slightly.

NUTRITION PER SERVE
Protein 1 g; Fat 18 g; Carbohydrate 28 g; Dietary Fibre 0 g; Cholesterol 51 mg; 1154 kJ (276 cal)

Use the best quality chocolate you can afford—it will make a huge difference.

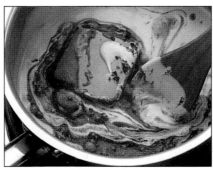

Put the sugar, butter and cream in a pan and stir until at boiling point.

Remove the pan from the heat before stirring in the rum and chocolate.

BERRY COULIS

Shown here with sorbet. Also good with fresh or poached fruit, soufflés, ice cream, pies and tarts.

Preparation time: 10 minutes
Total cooking time: Nil
Serves 6

250 g (8 oz) mixture of berries (strawberries, raspberries or blackberries)
2–4 tablespoons icing sugar, or to taste
1 tablespoon lemon juice
1–2 tablespoons Cointreau or Grand Marnier

1 Hull the berries. Place the fruit in a food processor and add the sugar and lemon juice. Blend until smooth. Stir in the Cointreau or Grand Marnier.

NUTRITION PER SERVE
Protein 1 g; Fat 0 g; Carbohydrate 16 g; Dietary Fibre 2 g; Cholesterol 0 mg; 317 kJ (76 cal)

COOK'S FILE

Variation: Make Mango Coulis using 2 mangoes, peeled, seeded and puréed, or frozen mango purée.

Hull the berries (remove the stalks and leaves from the fruit).

Put the fruit in a food processor or blender with the sugar and lemon juice.

Stir the liqueur into the blended coulis, adding as much or as little as you like.

Dips

TZATZIKI (MINTED CUCUMBER DIP)

Preparation time: 15 minutes
Total cooking time: Nil
Serves 4

1 Lebanese cucumber
2 cloves garlic, crushed
250 g (8 oz) plain yoghurt
1 teaspoon white vinegar
1 teaspoon chopped dill
1 teaspoon chopped mint

1 Finely grate the cucumber and squeeze out the excess moisture. Mix together in a bowl with the garlic, yoghurt, vinegar, fresh herbs and salt and freshly ground black pepper, to taste. Serve with pitta or Turkish bread or crudités.

NUTRITION PER SERVE
Protein 15 g; Fat 11 g; Carbohydrate 12 g; Dietary Fibre 0 g; Cholesterol 35 mg; 895 kJ (217 cal)

Use a large sharp knife to finely chop the fresh dill and mint.

Squeeze the excess moisture from the cucumber so the dip isn't watery.

Season the dip to taste with salt and pepper, then mix well.

Finely grate the rind and squeeze the juice from the fresh limes.

Cook the corn kernels briefly, then plunge into iced water, drain and pat dry.

Process the marinated prawns in short bursts until roughly chopped.

Mix together all the ingredients and leave in the fridge for 2 hours before serving.

PRAWN, CORN AND SWEET CHILLI DIP

Preparation time: 1 hour
 + 2 hours refrigeration
Total cooking time: 3 minutes
Serves 8

1 kg (2 lb) cooked prawns
juice and grated rind of 3 limes
100 g (3½ oz) frozen corn
    kernels
250 g (8 oz) soft cream cheese
¼ cup (15 g/½ oz) finely
    chopped chives
1 tablespoon sweet chilli sauce
4 cooked king prawns, to
    garnish

1 Peel, devein and rinse the prawns; pat them dry and place in a bowl. Add the lime juice to the prawns, cover and refrigerate for 10 minutes.

2 Cook the frozen corn kernels in boiling water for 2–3 minutes, or until tender. Drain and plunge the kernels into iced water to prevent further cooking, then drain and pat dry with paper towel.

3 Place the prawns and lime juice in a food processor and process in short bursts for 2–3 seconds until the prawns are chopped into small pieces but not minced.

4 Transfer the chopped prawns to a bowl and mix in the cream cheese, corn kernels, lime rind and chives. Add the chilli sauce and mix well. Cover the dip with plastic wrap and refrigerate for at least 2 hours. Just before serving, peel and devein the king prawns, leaving the tails intact. Transfer the dip to a serving bowl and garnish with the peeled prawns. Delicious served with a bowl of cooked king prawns, for dipping.

NUTRITION PER SERVE
Protein 35 g; Fat 12 g; Carbohydrate 5 g; Dietary Fibre 0 g; Cholesterol 280 mg; 1098 kJ (262 cal)

MARINATED ROASTED VEGETABLE DIP

Preparation time: 55 minutes
  + 4 hours marinating
Total cooking time: 50 minutes
Serves 8

1 small eggplant, sliced
2 zucchinis, sliced
1–2 tablespoons salt
3 red capsicums
1/2 cup (125 ml/4 fl oz) extra
  virgin olive oil
2 cloves garlic, sliced
2 Roma tomatoes
200 g (61/2 oz) canned, drained
  artichoke hearts
1/4 cup (7g/1/4 oz) oregano leaves
250 g (8 oz) ricotta cheese
1/4 cup (45 g/11/2 oz) sliced
  black olives

1 Place the eggplant and zucchini in a colander over a bowl and sprinkle with the salt, then leave to stand for 15–20 minutes. Meanwhile, cut the capsicums into large flat pieces, removing the seeds and membrane. Brush with a little of the olive oil and place, skin-side-up, under a hot grill until the skin blackens and blisters. Leave to cool under a tea towel or in a plastic bag, then peel away the skin. Reserve about a quarter of the capsicum to garnish and place the rest in a large non-metallic bowl.

2 Place half of the olive oil in a bowl, add 1 of the garlic cloves and a pinch of salt and mix together well. Rinse the eggplant and zucchini and pat dry with paper towels. Place the eggplant on a non-stick or foil-lined tray and brush with the garlic oil. Cook under a very hot grill for 4–6 minutes each side, or until golden brown, brushing both sides with the oil during grilling. The eggplant will burn easily, so keep a close watch. Allow to cool while grilling the zucchini in the same way. Add the eggplant and zucchini to the capsicum in the bowl.

3 Slice the tomatoes lengthwise, place on a non-stick or foil-lined baking tray and brush with the garlic oil. Reduce the temperature slightly and grill for 10–15 minutes, or until soft. Add to the bowl with the other vegetables.

4 Cut the artichokes into quarters and add to the bowl. Mix in any remaining garlic oil along with the remaining olive oil. Stir in the fresh oregano and remaining garlic. Cover with a tight-fitting lid or plastic wrap and refrigerate for at least 2 hours.

5 Drain the vegetables and place them in a food processor. Add the ricotta and process for 20 seconds, or until smooth. Reserve 1 tablespoon of olives to garnish and add the remainder to the food processor. Mix together in a couple of short bursts, then transfer to a non-metallic bowl and cover with plastic wrap. Chill for at least 2 hours.

6 Slice the reserved roasted red capsicum into fine strips and arrange over the top of the dip with the reserved olives.

NUTRITION PER SERVE
Protein 7 g; Fat 20 g; Carbohydrate 6 g; Dietary Fibre 3 g; Cholesterol 15 mg; 920 kJ (220 cal)

Slice the eggplant and zucchini, then place in a colander and sprinkle with salt.

Leave the capsicum to cool under a tea towel and the skin will peel away easily.

Add the grilled eggplant and zucchini to the roasted capsicum.

Slice the tomatoes lengthways, then brush with the garlic oil and grill until soft.

Add the fresh oregano leaves and the other clove of garlic to the vegetables.

Add the ricotta to the food processor and mix until the dip is smooth.

GUACAMOLE

Preparation time: 30 minutes
Total cooking time: Nil
Serves 6

3 ripe avocados
1 tablespoon lime or lemon juice
1 tomato
1–2 red chillies, finely chopped
1 small red onion, finely
   chopped
1 tablespoon finely chopped
   coriander leaves
2 tablespoons sour cream
1–2 drops Tabasco or habanero
   sauce

1 Roughly chop the avocado flesh and place in a bowl. Mash lightly with a fork and sprinkle with the lime or lemon juice to prevent the avocado discolouring.
2 Cut the tomato in half horizontally and use a teaspoon to scoop out the seeds. Finely dice the flesh and add to the avocado.
3 Stir in the chilli, onion, coriander, sour cream and Tabasco or habanero sauce. Season with freshly cracked black pepper.
4 Serve immediately or cover the surface with plastic wrap and refrigerate for 1–2 hours. If refrigerated, leave at room temperature for 15 minutes before serving.

NUTRITION PER SERVE
Protein 3 g; Fat 30 g; Carbohydrate 2 g; Dietary Fibre 3 g; Cholesterol 9 mg; 1200 kJ (290 cal)

COOK'S FILE

Hint: You will need 1–2 limes to produce 1 tablespoon of juice, depending on the lime. A heavier lime will probably be more juicy. To get more juice from a citrus fruit, prick it all over with a fork and then heat on High (100%) in the microwave for 1 minute. Don't forget to prick it or the fruit may burst.

Use disposable gloves when chopping chilli to avoid skin irritation.

Remove the avocado stone by chopping into it with a sharp knife and lifting up.

Cut the tomato in half horizontally and scoop out the seeds with a teaspoon.

You will only need a couple of drops of Tabasco or habanero—they are very hot.

ROASTED CAPSICUM AND CHILLI DIP

Preparation time: 40 minutes
+ 30 minutes refrigeration
Total cooking time: 35 minutes
Serves 8

2 large red capsicums
3 tablespoons olive oil
1–2 birds eye chillies
200 g (6½ oz) neufchatel cream
   cheese
3 tablespoons thick plain
   yoghurt
1 teaspoon red wine vinegar
½ teaspoon soft brown sugar
2 spring onions, chopped

1 Preheat the oven to moderately hot 200°C (400°F/Gas 6). Put the capsicums in a baking dish and drizzle with oil. Bake for 15 minutes. Make a small slit in each of the whole chillies (otherwise they will explode), add to the dish and bake for a further 20 minutes. (If the vegetables begin to burn, add about 1 tablespoon of water to the baking dish.) Allow to cool.
2 Peel the skin from the cooled capsicums. Cut them and the chillies in half and discard the seeds and membrane. Place the capsicum and chillies in a food processor and mix until pulpy.
3 Beat the cream cheese until soft, then add the capsicum chilli mixture, yoghurt, vinegar and sugar. Season to taste with salt and pepper, then cover and refrigerate for 30 minutes. Scatter with the spring onions to serve.

NUTRITION PER SERVE
Protein 4 g; Fat 15 g; Carbohydrate 4 g; Dietary Fibre 1 g; Cholesterol 23 mg; 675 kJ (160 cal)

Roast the capsicums for 15 minutes, then add the chillies.

Put the capsicum and chillies in a food processor and mix until pulpy.

Mix together all the ingredients, then refrigerate for 30 minutes before serving.

Quick dips

Dips are a wonderful treat for unfussy casual cooks, whose idea of culinary expertise is to rush into the kitchen and emerge with something quick but deliciously inventive. These recipes make great use of pantry staples and fridge leftovers, in a truly imaginative manner.

ROSEMARY AND CANNELLINI BEAN DIP

Mix a 400 g (13 oz) can rinsed and drained cannellini beans in a food processor with 1 crushed clove garlic, 2 teaspoons chopped rosemary and 1 tablespoon lemon juice for 1 minute. With the motor running, add 2 tablespoons extra virgin olive oil in a thin stream. Season and serve with crisp lavash bread or pitta chips. Serves 4.

NUTRITION PER SERVE
Protein 2 g; Fat 25 g; Carbohydrate 2 g; Dietary Fibre 0 g; Cholesterol 82 mg; 977 kJ (233 cal)

FRENCH ONION DIP

Use a fork to blend 250 g (8 oz) sour cream with a 30 g (1 oz) packet French onion soup mix. Cover and refrigerate for 1–2 hours. Serve with potato wedges, sweet potato chips or savoury biscuits. Serves 4.

NUTRITION PER SERVE
Protein 1 g; Fat 8 g; Carbohydrate 1 g; Dietary Fibre 0 g; Cholesterol 27 mg; 326 kJ (78 cal)

CREAMY TOMATO TUNA DIP

Mix 250 g (8 oz) soft cream cheese with a 100 g (6^1/2 oz) can tuna with tomato and onion (including the oil). Add black pepper, cover and refrigerate for 1–2 hours. Serve with sweet chilli chips, lavash bread or potato wedges. Serves 4.

NUTRITION PER SERVE
Protein 11 g; Fat 26 g; Carbohydrate 2 g; Dietary Fibre 0 g; Cholesterol 70 mg; 1185 kJ (283 cal)

MIXED HERB DIP

Chop 15 g (^{1}/2 oz) chives and mix with 1^1/4 cups (315 ml/ 10 fl oz) plain yoghurt. Add ^{1}/4 cup (7 g/^{1}/4 oz) marjoram leaves, ^{1}/4 cup (5 g/^{1}/4 oz) mint leaves and ^{1}/2 cup (10 g/^{1}/4 oz) flat-leaf parsley leaves. Season with black pepper. Serve with lavash bread, pitta or sweet chilli chips. Can also be made with thyme, oregano, garlic chives or dill. Serves 6.

NUTRITION PER SERVE
Protein 3 g; Fat 0 g; Carbohydrate 3 g; Dietary Fibre 0 g; Cholesterol 3 mg; 118 kJ (28 cal)

SWEET CHILLI
AND SOUR CREAM DIP

Mix 250 g (8 oz) sour cream with 3 tablespoons sweet chilli sauce. Swirl another teaspoon of sweet chilli sauce on top to decorate. Serve with herb and garlic pitta chips, goujons or sweet potato chips. Serves 4.

NUTRITION PER SERVE
Protein 2 g; Fat 25 g; Carbohydrate 10 g; Dietary Fibre 0 g; Cholesterol 82 mg; 1112 kJ (266 cal)

RED PESTO DIP

Mix together 250 g (8 oz) soft cream cheese, 2 tablespoons ready-made red pesto, 1 teaspoon lemon juice and 2 teaspoons chopped flat-leaf parsley. Season with black pepper and serve with herb and garlic pitta chips or savoury biscuits. Serves 4.

NUTRITION PER SERVE
Protein 7 g; Fat 23 g; Carbohydrate 6 g; Dietary Fibre 1 g; Cholesterol 61 mg; 1075 kJ (257 cal)

MUSTARD DIP

Mix together $^1/_2$ cup (125 g/4 fl oz) mayonnaise, $^1/_2$ cup (125 g/4 fl oz) plain yoghurt, 2 teaspoons Dijon mustard and 3 tablespoons wholegrain mustard. Season well and serve with chicken goujons or potato wedges. Serves 4.

NUTRITION PER SERVE
Protein 2 g; Fat 11 g; Carbohydrate 8 g; Dietary Fibre 0 g; Cholesterol 15 mg; 579 kJ (138 cal)

HUMMUS AND ORANGE DIP

Mix together 250 g (8 oz) hummus, 2 tablespoons orange juice, $^1/_4$ teaspoon ground cumin and 2 teaspoons chopped coriander. Season with freshly cracked black pepper and cover with plastic wrap. Refrigerate for 2–3 hours to develop the flavours. Serve with sweet potato chips, crisp lavash bread or pitta chips. Serves 4.

NUTRITION PER SERVE
Protein 6 g; Fat 11 g; Carbohydrate 7 g; Dietary Fibre 6 g; Cholesterol 0 mg; 606 kJ (145 cal)

Top, from left to right: Rosemary and Cannellini Bean; Creamy Tomato Tuna; Sweet Chilli and Sour Cream; Mustard.
Bottom, from left to right: French Onion; Mixed Herb; Red Pesto; Hummus and Orange.

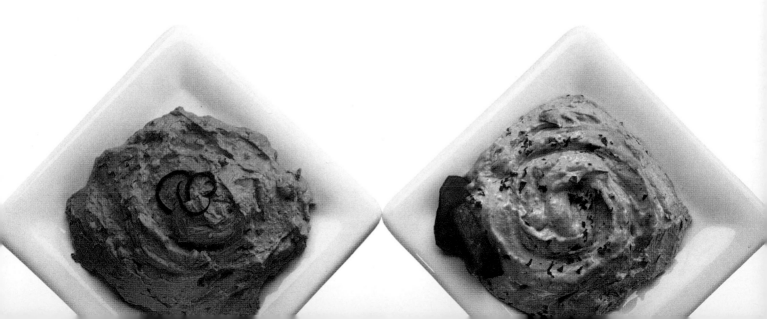

HUMMUS

Preparation time: 15 minutes
Total cooking time: Nil
Serves 4–6

425 g (14 oz) can chick peas
2–3 tablespoons lemon juice
2 tablespoons olive oil
2 cloves garlic, crushed
¼ cup (65 g/2¼ oz) tahini

1 Place the drained chick peas, lemon juice, olive oil and garlic in a food processor. Season with salt and pepper. Process for 20–30 seconds, or until smooth. Add the tahini and process for a further 10 seconds.

NUTRITION PER SERVE (6)
Protein 18 g; Fat 21 g; Carbohydrate 36 g;
Dietary Fibre 13 g; Cholesterol 0 mg;
1638 kJ (391 cal)

Drain the chick peas to get rid of the canning brine.

Process the chick peas, lemon juice, olive oil and garlic.

The hummus will be quite firm—if you prefer it softer, add a little water.

Put the dried chick peas in a bowl, cover with water and leave to rehydrate.

Simmer the chick peas for 45 minutes, skimming any scum from the surface.

Make sure the carrots are coated in the spices, then drizzle with honey.

Mash the carrot and spice mixture in the pan, to keep all the pan juices.

MOROCCAN SWEET CARROT AND HONEY DIP

Preparation time: 20 minutes
 + soaking overnight
Total cooking time: 1 hour
Serves 6

150 g (5 oz) dried chick peas
50 g (1³/4 oz) butter
¹/2 teaspoon ground cumin
¹/2 teaspoon ground coriander
¹/2 teaspoon ground cinnamon
¹/4 teaspoon chilli powder
200 g (6¹/2 oz) carrots, chopped
1 tablespoon honey
¹/3 cup (80 ml/2³/4 oz) thick
  natural yoghurt
2 tablespoons chopped parsley
2 tablespoons olive oil
1 tablespoon olive oil, extra

1 Place the chick peas in a bowl, cover with water and soak overnight. Drain and rinse well, then place in a saucepan and cover with cold water. Bring to the boil, reduce the heat and simmer for 45 minutes or until tender. Skim off any scum that rises to the surface. Drain, rinse and mash well.
2 Melt the butter in a heavy-based frying pan; add the cumin, coriander, cinnamon, chilli and carrots. Cook, covered, over low heat for 5 minutes, turning the carrots to coat them in the spices. Drizzle with honey. If the carrots start to stick add 1 tablespoon water. Cover and cook for 20 minutes until the carrots are very tender and a caramel brown colour. Cool slightly and mash in the frying pan to include all the bits on the base of the pan.
3 Combine the mashed chick pea and carrot, with the yoghurt, parsley and olive oil, and season well with salt and pepper. Spoon into a serving bowl and drizzle with extra oil. Serve with celery sticks or blanched green beans.

NUTRITION PER SERVE
Protein 6 g; Fat 20 g; Carbohydrate 20 g; Dietary Fibre 5 g; Cholesterol 24 mg; 1087 kJ (260 cal)

COOK'S FILE

Note: If you use canned chick peas the cooking time will be much shorter but the flavour not quite as good.

TARAMASALATA

Preparation time: 25 minutes
Total cooking time: Nil
Serves 8

4 slices white bread, crusts
   removed
1/4 cup (60 ml/2 fl oz) milk
100 g (31/2 oz) smoked cod's roe
   (tarama)
1 egg yolk
1 clove garlic, crushed
1 tablespoon grated onion
1/4 cup (60 ml/2 fl oz) olive oil
1/3 cup (80 ml/23/4 fl oz) lemon
   juice

1 Soak the bread slices in the milk for 5 minutes, then remove and squeeze out the excess liquid.
2 Process the cod's roe and egg yolk in a food processor for 10 seconds. Add the bread, garlic and onion and process for 20 seconds, or until the mixture is well combined and smooth.
3 With the motor running, gradually add the olive oil in a thin stream. Process until all the oil is absorbed.
4 Add the lemon juice in small amounts, to taste. Transfer to a bowl and serve with bread and black olives.

NUTRITION PER SERVE
Protein 7 g; Fat 9 g; Carbohydrate 14 g; Dietary Fibre 1 g; Cholesterol 125 mg; 699 kJ (167 cal)

COOK'S FILE

Note: As shop-bought taramasalata is usually bright pink, you might expect this dish to be. The pinkness will depend on the type of cod's roe you buy, but this classic Greek dish only has a slight hint of colour. Smoked cod's roe is available from most delicatessens and fishmongers and also Greek food stores. Roe of grey mullet can also be used.
Storage: Refrigerate in an airtight container, for up to 1 week. Bring to room temperature before serving.

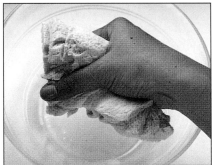

Leave the bread to soak in the milk, then squeeze out the excess liquid.

Add the bread, garlic and grated onion to the processed roe and egg yolk.

Add the olive oil to the mixture in a thin stream, with the motor running.

Add the lemon juice a little at a time until you have reached the right tartness.

74

ASPARAGUS, APPLE AND AVOCADO DIP

Preparation time: 40 minutes
+ 2 hours refrigeration
Total cooking time: 5 minutes
Serves 10–12

2 bunches asparagus
3 green apples
2 tablespoons lemon juice
3 ripe avocados
300 g (10 oz) sour cream
4 drops Tabasco sauce

1 Wash and trim the woody ends from the asparagus. Steam or microwave until just cooked, then plunge into iced water and drain. Chop off the tips and set aside, to serve. Finely chop the remaining asparagus stalks.

2 Peel and grate the apples and sprinkle with 1 tablespoon lemon juice to prevent browning. Add the asparagus and mix together. In a separate dish, mash the avocado flesh. Mix in the remaining lemon juice and stir into the apple and asparagus. Add the sour cream and mix well. Add the Tabasco, cover with plastic wrap and refrigerate for 2 hours. Serve with the asparagus tips for dipping.

NUTRITION PER SERVE (12)
Protein 2 g; Fat 24 g; Carbohydrate 7 g; Dietary Fibre 2 g; Cholesterol 33 mg; 1024 kJ (245 cal)

Remove the woody ends from the asparagus by snapping with your fingers.

As soon as you have grated the apple, sprinkle with lemon juice.

You will only need a little Tabasco to add spiciness to the dip.

Dippers

Rather than serving up a plate of tired pitta bread with your wonderful array of dips,
why not spend a little time making a platter of irresistibly crunchy dippers? Our only advice
with these recipes is to make a large quantity... people tend to come back for more.

HERB AND GARLIC PITTA CHIPS

Slice 2 Lebanese pitta breads in half. Mix together 100 g
(3 1/2 oz) butter, 4 crushed cloves garlic, 1 tablespoon
chopped thyme, 2 teaspoons chopped marjoram and
2 teaspoons chopped rosemary. Spread over the pitta and
cut into 6–8 triangles. Bake at moderate 180°C (350°F/
Gas 4) for 5–10 minutes, or until crisp and golden. Store for
up to a day in an airtight container and, if necessary, crisp
up in the oven for a few minutes. Serves 2–4.

NUTRITION PER SERVE (4)
Protein 3 g; Fat 20 g; Carbohydrate 16 g; Dietary Fibre 1 g;
Cholesterol 64 mg; 1110 kJ (265 cal)

CRISP LAVASH BREAD

Lightly brush 3 pieces of lavash bread with olive oil and
sprinkle with 1–2 teaspoons sea salt flakes. Cut each piece
into 6 strips, and each strip into 4 rectangles. Bake at
moderate 180°C (350°F/Gas 4) for 10–15 minutes, or until
crisp and lightly browned. Can be stored for 1–2 days in an
airtight container. Serves 4–6.

NUTRITION PER SERVE (6)
Protein 4 g; Fat 10 g; Carbohydrate 21 g; Dietary Fibre 2 g;
Cholesterol 0 mg; 800 kJ (191 cal)

SPICY CHICKEN GOUJONS

Cut 3 chicken breasts into thin strips and toss in plain flour,
shaking off the excess. Half fill a deep pan with oil and heat
until moderately hot. Gently lower the goujons into the oil, a
few at a time, and fry for 2–3 minutes or until golden. Drain
and keep warm. Mix together a teaspoon of salt,
1/2 teaspoon ground turmeric, 1/2 teaspoon ground coriander,
1/2 teaspoon ground cumin and 1/2 teaspoon chilli powder.
Toss the goujons in the mixture, shaking off the excess.
Serve with a creamy dip or sweet chilli sauce. Serves 2–4.

NUTRITION PER SERVE (4)
Protein 29 g; Fat 31 g; Carbohydrate 11 g; Dietary Fibre 1 g;
Cholesterol 60 mg; 1838 kJ (439 cal)

CORN CHIPS

Cut 4 corn tortillas into eight pieces. Half fill a heavy-based
pan with oil and heat until moderately hot (a small bread
cube should sizzle and turn golden brown if the oil is
ready). Cook the corn tortillas in batches for 1–2 minutes, or
until crisp and golden. Drain on paper towels. Serves 2–4.

NUTRITION PER SERVE (4)
Protein 4 g; Fat 10 g; Carbohydrate 15 g; Dietary Fibre 2 g;
Cholesterol 1 mg; 810 kJ (205 cal)

POTATO SKINS

Scrub 5 or 6 large potatoes and pat dry with paper towels but do not peel. Prick each potato with a fork. Bake at hot 210°C (415°F/Gas 6–7) for 1 hour, or until the skins are crisp and the flesh is soft. Turn once during cooking. Leave the potatoes to cool, then halve them and scoop out the flesh, leaving a thin layer of potato in each shell. Cut each half into 3 wedges. Half fill a heavy-based pan with oil and heat to moderately hot. Cook the potato skins in batches for 2–3 minutes, or until crisp. Drain on paper towels. Sprinkle with salt and cracked black pepper and serve with a creamy dip or a salsa. Serves 2–4.

NUTRITION PER SERVE (4)
Protein 6 g; Fat 30 g; Carbohydrate 63 g; Dietary Fibre 7 g;
Cholesterol 0 mg; 2221 kJ (531 cal)

SWEET POTATO CHIPS

Peel 2 orange sweet potatoes and slice as thinly as possible. Half fill a deep pan with oil and heat until moderately hot (a small bread cube should sizzle and turn golden brown if the oil is ready). Deep-fry the sweet potato chips in small batches until crisp and golden (don't overload the pan or they will stick together). Remove with a slotted spoon and drain on paper towels. Lightly sprinkle with salt. Serve immediately with sweet chilli sauce. Serves 2–4.

NUTRITION PER SERVE (4)
Protein 3 g; Fat 29 g; Carbohydrate 25 g; Dietary Fibre 3 g;
Cholesterol 0 mg; 1532 kJ (366 cal)

SWEET CHILLI CHIPS

Divide 4 Lebanese pitta breads in half, then cut into small triangles. Line 3 baking trays with baking paper, arrange the triangles on the baking trays and brush each side generously with sweet chilli sauce (you will need about 1 cup (250 ml/8 fl oz). Bake at very slow 140°C (275°F/Gas 1), turning once, for 5–10 minutes, or until the chips are golden brown on both sides. Can be stored for 1–2 days in an airtight container. Serves 4–6.

NUTRITION PER SERVE (6)
Protein 4 g; Fat 1 g; Carbohydrate 43 g; Dietary Fibre 2 g;
Cholesterol 0 mg; 812 kJ (194 cal)

PESTO BAGEL CHIPS

Slice 4 three-day old plain bagels into 6 thin rings. Bake on a baking tray at warm 170°C (325°F/Gas 3) for 10 minutes. Brush with pesto and sprinkle with shredded Parmesan. Bake for 5 minutes, or until lightly golden. Serves 2–4.

NUTRITION PER SERVE (4)
Protein 9 g; Fat 3 g; Carbohydrate 45 g; Dietary Fibre 3 g;
Cholesterol 0 mg; 1044 kJ (250 cal)

Top, from left: Herb and Garlic Pitta Chips; Spicy Chicken Goujons; Potato Skins; Sweet Chilli Chips. Bottom, from left: Crisp Lavash Bread; Corn Chips; Sweet Potato Chips; Pesto Bagel Chips.

SMOKED TROUT DIP

Preparation time: 25 minutes
Total cooking time: Nil
Serves 4

250 g (8 oz) smoked trout
1½ teaspoons light olive oil
½ cup (125 ml/4 fl oz) cream
1 tablespoon lemon juice
pinch of cayenne pepper
1 tablespoon pistachio nuts
1 tablespoon parsley leaves

1 Remove the skin and bone from the trout and flake the flesh. Place the flesh in a blender or food processor and add the olive oil, 2 teaspoons of the cream and the lemon juice. Blend until the mixture forms a thick paste. Add the remaining cream, a little at a time, then season with salt and the cayenne pepper. Transfer to a serving bowl.
2 Combine the pistachios and parsley and chop finely. Sprinkle over the top of the dip to serve. Delicious with witlof leaves or cucumber sticks.

NUTRITION PER SERVE
Protein 17 g; Fat 22 g; Carbohydrate 1 g; Dietary Fibre 1 g; Cholesterol 91 mg; 1115 kJ (226 cal)

COOK'S FILE

Hint: Add the cream a little at a time and take care not to overwork in the processor or it will curdle.

Peel the skin from the fish and then carefully remove the backbone.

Mix the trout flesh to a thick paste with the oil, cream and lemon juice.

Mix together the pistachios and parsley, then chop well to make a garnish.

WHITE BEAN, CHICK PEA AND HERB DIP

Preparation time: 20 minutes
 + overnight soaking
Total cooking time: 1 hour
Serves 10–12

180 g (6 oz) dried cannellini
 beans
100 g (3½ oz) dried chick peas
3 slices white bread
3 tablespoons milk
2 spring onions, finely chopped
4 tablespoons thick plain
 yoghurt
1 tablespoon lemon juice
2 teaspoons finely grated lemon
 rind
1 tablespoon chopped parsley
2 teaspoons chopped oregano
2 tablespoons olive oil

1 Soak the beans and chick peas in cold water overnight. Rinse well and transfer to a pan. Cover with cold water and bring to the boil. Reduce the heat and simmer for 1 hour, or until very tender, adding more water if needed. Skim any froth from the surface. Drain well, cool and mash.

2 Remove the crusts from the bread, place in a bowl and drizzle with the milk. Leave for 2 minutes, then mash with your fingertips until very soft. Mix together with the beans.

3 Add the spring onion, yoghurt, lemon juice, rind, fresh herbs and oil and season well. Mix together well and serve at room temperature.

NUTRITION PER SERVE (12)
Protein 4 g; Fat 4 g; Carbohydrate 12 g;
Dietary Fibre 2 g; Cholesterol 2 mg;
416 kJ (99 cal)

Simmer the beans and chick peas for an hour, skimming froth from the surface.

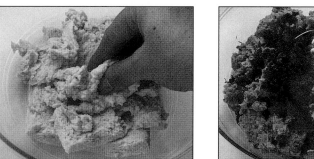

Soak the bread in the milk for 2 minutes, then mash up with your fingertips.

Add the spring onion, yoghurt, herbs, oil, lemon juice, rind and seasoning.

CHILLI CON QUESO

Preparation time: 25 minutes
Total cooking time: 15 minutes
Serves 6

2 green jalapeno chillies
30 g (1 oz) butter
1 onion, finely chopped
3/4 cup (185 g/6 oz) sour cream
250 g (8 oz) grated Cheddar

1 Roast the chillies by holding them with tongs (one at a time) over a gas flame, until well blackened (or, if you don't have gas, cut the chillies in half, remove the seeds, flatten out and grill until the skin turns black). Place in a plastic bag and set aside to cool. Scrape away the skin, remove the seeds and finely chop the flesh.

2 Melt the butter in a small pan. Add the onion and cook over low heat for 5 minutes, or until softened and lightly golden. Add the chilli and stir to combine.

3 Add the sour cream and stir until the cream has warmed and thinned down slightly. Add the Cheddar cheese and keep stirring until it has melted and the mixture is smooth. Great with potato skins or corn chips.

NUTRITION PER SERVE
Protein 12 g; Fat 30 g; Carbohydrate 2 g;
Dietary Fibre 0 g; Cholesterol 95 mg;
1360 kJ (325 cal)

An easy way to remove the skins from chillies is to hold them over a gas flame.

Cook the onion until soft and lightly golden, then add the chopped chilli.

Add the cheese and continue stirring until it has melted and the dip is smooth.

To thoroughly clean a leek, split with a knife and hold under running water.

Cook the leek for 15 minutes, adding the garlic for the last 5 minutes.

LEEK AND SORREL DIP

Preparation time: 35 minutes
Total cooking time: 20 minutes
Serves 8

50 g (1¾ oz) butter
2 leeks, chopped
3 cloves garlic, crushed
1 cup (60 g/2 oz) shredded
  sorrel leaves
1 teaspoon ground cumin
½ cup (125 g/4 oz) ricotta
½ cup (125 g/4 oz) sour
  cream

1 tablespoon lemon juice
1 tablespoon sesame seeds,
  toasted

1 Melt the butter in a large frying pan that has a lid. Add the leek and stir well. Cover and cook over low heat for 15 minutes, or until very soft. Make sure that the leek does not burn. During the last 5 minutes of cooking, add the garlic and stir well.
2 Add the sorrel and cumin and cook for another minute. Remove from the heat and allow to cool.
3 Place in a food processor with the ricotta, sour cream and lemon juice and process for 15 seconds, or until smooth. Season with salt and pepper and scatter with the toasted sesame seeds to serve.

NUTRITION PER SERVE
Protein 4 g; Fat 15 g; Carbohydrate 4 g; Dietary Fibre 3 g; Cholesterol 44 mg; 687 kJ (164 cal)

Add the shredded sorrel leaves and the cumin and cook for another minute.

Blend in a food processor with the ricotta, sour cream and lemon juice.

C O O K ' S   F I L E

Hint: Always wash leeks very well before cooking as the compact layers can harbour a lot of grit.

MEXICAN LAYERED DIP

Preparation time: 50 minutes
Total cooking time: Nil
Serves 12

450 g (14 oz) can refried beans
35 g (1¼ oz) packet of taco
    seasoning mix
300 g (10 oz) sour cream
200 g (6½ oz) ready-made salsa
    sauce
½ cup (60 g/2 oz) grated
    Cheddar
2 tablespoons chopped pitted
    black olives
200 g (6½ oz) corn chips
1 tablespoon chopped coriander

Guacamole
3 ripe avocados
1 tomato
1–2 red chillies, finely chopped
1 small red onion, finely
    chopped
1 tablespoon chopped coriander
1 tablespoon lime or lemon juice
2 tablespoons sour cream
1–2 drops habanero sauce or
    Tabasco sauce

1 Using a fork, mix the refried beans and taco seasoning together in a small bowl.
2 To make the guacamole, cut the avocados in half, peel and discard the skin and stone (chop into the stone with a sharp knife and lift it out). Roughly chop the avocados and place in a bowl, then mash lightly with a fork. Cut the tomato in half horizontally, scoop out the seeds with a teaspoon and discard. Finely dice the flesh and add to the avocado. Stir in the chilli, onion, coriander, lime or lemon juice, sour cream and habanero or Tabasco sauce. Season with freshly cracked black pepper.
3 To assemble, spread the bean mixture in the middle of a large serving platter (we used a 30 x 35 cm/ 12 x 14 inch dish), leaving a clear border for the corn chips. Spoon the sour cream on top, leaving a small border of bean mixture showing. repeat with the guacamole and salsa sauce so that you can see each layer. Sprinkle with cheese and olives.
4 Arrange the corn chips around the edge of the platter just before serving and garnish with the coriander.

NUTRITION PER SERVE
Protein 27 g; Fat 36 g; Carbohydrate 73 g; Dietary Fibre 25 g; Cholesterol 42 mg; 2982 kJ (550 cal)

COOK'S FILE

Note: Habanero sauce is a very hot condiment sauce made from habanero chillies. Use sparingly to add extra zing to the dip. It is available from delicatessens and speciality stores.
Hint: Always try to wear rubber gloves when you are chopping chillies. If this isn't possible, remember to scrub your hands thoroughly with warm soapy water after chopping. Be careful not to touch your eyes or any other delicate skin or you will cause burning and skin irritation.
Storage: The dip can be made 1–2 hours in advance and refrigerated, covered with plastic wrap.

Mash together the refried beans and the taco seasoning mix.

Remove the skin and stone from the avocado and mash the flesh.

Scoop out the seeds from the tomato and dice the flesh.

Season the guacamole with freshly ground black pepper.

Build up the layers of the dip, leaving a border around each so they can be seen.

Sprinkle the top of the layered dip with the grated cheese and chopped olives.

83

ARTICHOKE DIP

Preparation time: 10 minutes
Total cooking time: 15 minutes
Serves 8

**2 x 400 g (13 oz) cans artichoke
hearts, drained
1 cup (250 g/8 oz) mayonnaise
3/4 cup (75 g/2 1/2 oz) grated
Parmesan
2 teaspoons onion flakes
2 tablespoons grated Parmesan,
extra
paprika, to sprinkle**

1 Preheat the oven to moderate 180°C
(350°F/Gas 4). Gently squeeze the
artichokes to remove any remaining
liquid. Chop and place in a bowl. Stir
through the mayonnaise, Parmesan
and onion flakes.
2 Spread into a 1-litre capacity
shallow ovenproof dish. Sprinkle with
the extra Parmesan and a little
paprika. Bake for 15 minutes, or until
heated through and lightly browned
on top. Serve with crusty bread.

NUTRITION PER SERVE
Protein 7 g; Fat 14 g; Carbohydrate 8 g;
Dietary Fibre 3 g; Cholesterol 21 mg;
773 kJ (185 cal)

COOK'S FILE

Note: Use the mayonnaise recipe on
page 24 for a great flavour, or ready-
made mayonnaise if time is short.

*Gently squeeze the artichoke hearts to
remove any remaining liquid.*

*Mix the chopped artichoke with the
mayonnaise, Parmesan and onion flakes.*

*Spread the dip in a shallow dish and
sprinkle with Parmesan and paprika.*

BABA GANOUJ (EGGPLANT DIP)

Preparation time: 15 minutes
+ 20 minutes standing
Total cooking time: 35 minutes
Serves 6–8

2 medium eggplants
3–4 cloves garlic, crushed
2 tablespoons lemon juice
2 tablespoons tahini
1 tablespoon olive oil
sprinkle of paprika, to garnish

1 Halve the eggplants lengthways, sprinkle with salt and leave to stand for 15–20 minutes. Rinse and pat dry with paper towels. Preheat the oven to moderate 180°C (350°F/Gas 4).
2 Bake the eggplants for 35 minutes, or until soft. Peel away the skin and discard. Place the flesh in a food processor with the garlic, lemon juice, tahini and olive oil and season to taste with salt and pepper. Process for 20–30 seconds. Sprinkle with paprika and serve with Lebanese bread.

NUTRITION PER SERVE (8)
Protein 2 g; Fat 6 g; Carbohydrate 2 g; Dietary Fibre 3 g; Cholesterol 0 mg; 288 kJ (70 cal)

COOK'S FILE

Note: We sprinkle eggplants with salt and leave them before using because they can have a bitter taste. The salt draws the bitter liquid from the eggplant. Slender eggplants do not need to be treated before use.

Tahini is a paste made from crushed sesame seeds.

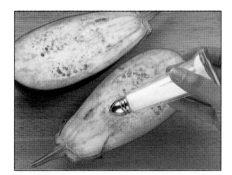

Sprinkle the eggplant with salt to remove any bitterness.

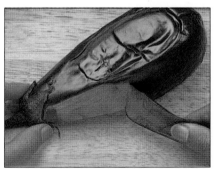

Once the eggplant has been roasted, the skin will peel away easily.

Process the eggplant with the garlic, lemon juice, tahini and olive oil.

MOULDED EGG AND CAVIAR DIP

Preparation time: 1 hour
+ 2 hours refrigeration
Total cooking time: 6 minutes
Serves 10–12

7 eggs (see Note)
3 tablespoons finely chopped
  parsley
3 tablespoons whole egg
  mayonnaise
2 bunches chives, finely
  chopped
500 g (1 lb) cream cheese,
  softened to room temperature
90 g (3 oz) jar black caviar
300 g (10 oz) sour cream
extra chives and black caviar, to
  serve

1 Fill a pan with cold water and gently add the eggs. Bring to the boil, then reduce the heat and simmer for 6 minutes. Drain and plunge the eggs in cold water to stop the cooking process. Cool thoroughly and drain.
2 Line a deep loose-based fluted flan tin (about 18 cm/7 inches across) with plastic wrap, leaving a wide overhang to help you remove the moulded dip from the tin.
3 Peel and mash the eggs, add the parsley and mayonnaise, and season with salt and pepper, to taste.
4 Divide the egg mixture in half.

Spoon one half into the lined tin. Firmly press down and smooth the surface with a spatula or the back of a spoon, pressing well into the side of the tin. Sprinkle with half the chives, pressing them down into the dip. Using a clean, warm spatula, spread over half the cream cheese to form another layer. Spoon over half the caviar and press down gently.
5 Repeat the layering with the remaining egg mixture, chives, cream cheese and caviar. Cover the moulded dip with plastic wrap, pressing down firmly so the layers stick together, and refrigerate for 2 hours.
6 Remove the top cover of plastic wrap and place a plate over the mould. Flip over onto the plate while holding the tin and gently ease the tin off. Remove the plastic wrap, trying not to damage the fluted edges.
7 Spoon dollops of the sour cream over the top of the mould and spread a little. Decorate with the extra snipped chives and a few spoonfuls of caviar. Serve with water crackers.

NUTRITION PER SERVE (12)
Protein 10 g; Fat 30 g; Carbohydrate 3 g; Dietary Fibre 0 g; Cholesterol 217 mg; 1620 kJ (387 cal)

C O O K ' S F I L E

Note: A little forward planning is very useful for this recipe: eggs at room temperature are less likely to crack when boiled. The cream cheese will be much easier to spread if it is left to soften at room temperature.

  The flavour of the dip will be much better if you use home-made mayonnaise (page 24).
Variation: This is a dip for a special occasion, but you can also prepare it using cod's roe or finely chopped smoked salmon instead of the caviar.

Even though you are using a loose-based tin, it is best to line it as well.

Mash the eggs in a bowl and add the parsley and mayonnaise.

Spread half the softened cream cheese over the egg layer.

Repeat the layers, spreading the egg layer over the caviar.

Gently ease the side of the tin away from the moulded dip.

Remove the plastic wrap carefully, trying not to damage the fluted edge.

CREAMY BLUE CHEESE DIP WITH PEARS

Preparation time: 25 minutes
+ 20 minutes refrigeration
Total cooking time: Nil
Serves 4

150 g (5 oz) creamy blue cheese
200 ml (6½ fl oz) thick cream
3 tablespoons thick plain
  yoghurt
2 tablespoons finely chopped
  chives
4 ripe pears, cored and cut into
  wedges

1 Mash the blue cheese with a fork to soften it slightly. Add the cream and yoghurt and season with freshly ground black pepper, mixing until smooth and well blended—do not overmix or it will become grainy and curdled. Spoon into a serving bowl, cover and refrigerate for 20 minutes, or until firm.
2 Scatter the chives over the dip. Serve with the pear wedges.

NUTRITION PER SERVE
Protein 10 g; Fat 30 g; Carbohydrate 45 g; Dietary Fibre 8 g; Cholesterol 100 mg; 2042 kJ (488 cal)

COOK'S FILE

Note: A creamy cheese such as Dolcelatte, Gorgonzola or King Island Blue will give the best result.

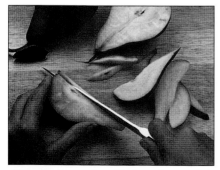

Use ripe pears for dipping. Any variety will suit—we used beurre bosc.

Mash the blue cheese with a fork to soften it slightly.

Add the cream and yoghurt and season to taste with ground black pepper.

CHILLI CRAB AND TOMATO DIP

Preparation time: 25 minutes
Total cooking time: Nil
Serves 6

2 x 170 g (5½ oz) cans crab meat, drained
200 g (6½ oz) neufchatel cheese (see Note)
2 tablespoons chilli sauce
2 teaspoons tomato paste
1 teaspoon grated lemon rind
2 teaspoons lemon juice
1 small onion, finely grated
3 spring onions, finely sliced
1 tomato, seeded and finely chopped

1 Squeeze any remaining liquid from the crab meat. Beat the neufchatel until smooth, then add the crab meat, chilli sauce, tomato paste, lemon rind, lemon juice and onion. Season well with salt and pepper. Mix together well and spoon into a serving bowl.
2 Scatter the spring onion and chopped tomato over the top and chill before serving.

NUTRITION PER SERVE
Protein 11 g; Fat 11 g; Carbohydrate 6 g; Dietary Fibre 1 g; Cholesterol 79 mg; 682 kJ (163 cal)

COOK'S FILE

Note: Neufchatel is a smooth, mild, good-quality cream cheese available from delicatessens.

Squeeze any remaining liquid from the crab or the dip will be watery.

Beat the neufchatel cheese with a wooden spoon until it is smooth.

Add the crab meat, chilli sauce, tomato paste, lemon rind and juice, and onion.

Salsas

PEACH, RED CAPSICUM AND GINGER SALSA

Shown here with chargrilled chicken breast. Good with seafood and barbecued meats.

Preparation time: 20 minutes
Total cooking time: Nil
Serves 4

3 tablespoons white wine vinegar
2 tablespoons caster sugar
2 teaspoons grated fresh ginger
1 clove garlic, crushed
1/2 teaspoon ground cumin
1/4 cup (15 g/1/2 oz) chopped
 coriander leaves
1/4 cup (15 g/1/2 oz) chopped
 mint
1 red capsicum, diced
1 small red onion, finely diced
1 small red chilli, finely chopped
3 canned or fresh peaches,
 diced

1 Combine the vinegar, sugar, ginger, garlic, cumin, coriander and mint.
2 Put the capsicum, onion, chilli and peaches in a large bowl. Gently stir through the vinegar herb mixture and serve at once.

NUTRITION PER SERVE
Protein 2 g; Fat 0 g; Carbohydrate 24 g;
Dietary Fibre 3 g; Cholesterol 0 mg;
454 kJ (108 cal)

Use fresh peaches if they are in season, otherwise canned will suffice.

Mix together the vinegar, sugar, ginger, garlic, cumin, coriander and mint.

Stir through the vinegar herb mixture and serve at once.

MELON SALSA

Shown here with white fish fillet. Also good with chicken, squid, lobster, prawns, pan-fried veal and pork.

Preparation time: 25 minutes
+ 1 hour refrigeration
Total cooking time: Nil
Serves 6–8

1/2 **honeydew melon (weighing about 750 g/1 1/2 lb)**
1 **red onion**
2 **small red chillies**
3 **tablespoons finely chopped coriander leaves**
2 **tablespoons lime juice**

1 Dice the melon and finely chop the onion. Wearing plastic gloves, cut the chillies in half. Remove the membrane and seeds and finely chop the flesh.
2 Place the melon, onion, chillies and coriander in a large bowl. Add the lime juice; mix well and cover with plastic wrap. Refrigerate for 1 hour to let the flavours develop.

NUTRITION PER SERVE (8)
Protein 1 g; Fat 0 g; Carbohydrate 7 g; Dietary Fibre 1 g; Cholesterol 0 mg; 135 kJ (32 cal)

Cut the melon flesh into small, evenly sized dice.

Use disposable gloves to de-seed the chillies, to avoid skin irritation.

Add the lime juice to the salsa, mix well and leave for 1 hour before serving.

CHARGRILLED VEGETABLE SALSA

Shown here with polenta wedges. Also good with barbecued or grilled meat or chicken.

Preparation time: 30 minutes
  + 2 hours marinating
Total cooking time: 30 minutes
Serves 4

2 Roma tomatoes
1 small red capsicum
1 small green capsicum
2 small zucchini
2 slender eggplants
3 tablespoons olive oil
1 tablespoon chopped flat-leaf
  parsley
2 teaspoons chopped marjoram
2 teaspoons chopped oregano
2 tablespoons balsamic vinegar
1 tablespoon chopped flat-leaf
  parsley, extra
2 teaspoons chopped marjoram,
  extra

1 Halve the tomatoes, capsicums, zucchini and eggplants lengthways. Place in a large shallow dish and pour over the combined olive oil and herbs. Toss well and leave to marinate for at least 2 hours or up to a day.
2 Heat the barbecue or chargrill pan and cook the vegetables until soft and a little blackened. Place the capsicum

in a plastic bag for a few minutes, then peel away the skin. Cut all the vegetables into small pieces and mix with the vinegar and extra herbs.

NUTRITION PER SERVE
Protein 3 g; Fat 15 g; Carbohydrate 7 g; Dietary Fibre 5 g; Cholesterol 0 mg; 733 kJ (175 cal)

Cut the tomatoes, capsicums, zucchini and eggplants in half lengthways.

Barbecue or chargrill the vegetables until soft and a little blackened.

Cut the vegetables into small chunks and mix with the herbs and vinegar.

SMOKED SALMON AND AVOCADO SALSA

Shown here on bruschetta. Also good with baked potatoes and other salads.

Preparation time: 15 minutes
Total cooking time: Nil
Serves 4–6

200 g (6½ oz) smoked salmon, cut into thin strips
4 spring onions, finely chopped
½ cup (30 g/1 oz) finely chopped parsley
1 tablespoon baby capers, washed and drained
1 large avocado, diced

1 teaspoon grated lime rind
3 tablespoons lime juice

1 Combine the salmon, spring onion, parsley and capers in a bowl. Keep refrigerated until required.
2 Just prior to serving, gently fold through the avocado and the combined lime rind and juice.

NUTRITION PER SERVE (6)
Protein 9 g; Fat 11 g; Carbohydrate 1 g; Dietary Fibre 1 g; Cholesterol 16 mg; 555 kJ (133 cal)

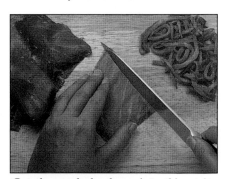

Cut the smoked salmon into thin strips with a sharp knife.

Rinse and drain the capers to wash off the brine.

Gently fold through the avocado and lime rind and juice.

PUMPKIN SEED SALSA

Shown here with crumbed fish fillets. Also good with chargrilled chicken or barbecued meats.

Preparation time: 15 minutes
Total cooking time: 20 minutes
Serves 6–8

160 g (5½ oz) pumpkin seeds (pepitas)
2 corn cobs
4 tablespoons lime juice
300 g (10 oz) Roma tomatoes, diced
1 teaspoon ground cumin
1–2 jalapeno chillies, finely chopped

1 Dry-fry the pumpkin seeds over medium heat, stirring occasionally, for 3–4 minutes or until puffed.
2 Brush the corn with some of the lime juice, then roast under a grill for 15–20 minutes, or until tender. Set aside until cool enough to handle, then slice off the kernels.
3 Mix the corn with the pumpkin seeds, tomato, cumin and chilli. Season well with salt and lots of coarsely ground pepper, then add the remaining lime juice and mix well.

NUTRITION PER SERVE (8)
Protein 5 g; Fat 10 g; Carbohydrate 10 g; Dietary Fibre 3 g; Cholesterol 0 mg; 640 kJ (155 cal)

Toast the pumpkin seeds in a dry frying pan until they are puffed.

Grill the corn cobs until lightly browned and tender, then slice off the kernels.

Mix together all the ingredients and season well with salt and pepper.

BOCCONCINI, TOMATO AND SUN-DRIED CAPSICUM SALSA

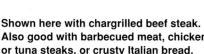

Shown here with chargrilled beef steak. Also good with barbecued meat, chicken or tuna steaks, or crusty Italian bread.

Preparation time: 20 minutes
Total cooking time: Nil
Serves 6

180 g (6 oz) bocconcini, diced
200 g (6¹/2 oz) tomatoes, diced
¹/3 cup (50 g/1³/4 oz) drained
    sun-dried capsicum in oil,
    chopped
1 spring onion, finely sliced
1 tablespoon extra virgin olive
    oil
2 teaspoons red wine vinegar
1 tablespoon shredded basil
    leaves
1 tablespoon chopped flat-leaf
    parsley

1 Mix together the bocconcini, tomato, sun-dried capsicum and spring onion in a large bowl.
2 Whisk together the oil and vinegar until thoroughly blended. Stir through the basil and parsley.
3 Toss the dressing through the bocconcini and tomato mixture and season to taste with salt and black pepper. Serve at room temperature.

NUTRITION PER SERVE
Protein 8 g; Fat 13 g; Carbohydrate 1 g; Dietary Fibre 1 g; Cholesterol 19 mg; 644 kJ (154 cal)

C O O K ' S   F I L E

Note: Bocconcini are small, fresh mozzarella cheeses.

Cut the bocconcini cheese and tomatoes into small dice.

Mix together the bocconcini, tomato, capsicum and spring onion.

Stir the basil and flat-leaf parsley into the vinaigrette dressing.

PINEAPPLE SALSA

Shown here with grilled swordfish kebabs. Also good with grilled chicken or fish.

Preparation time: 20 minutes
+ 2 hours standing
Total cooking time: Nil
Serves 8

375 g (12 oz) pineapple, diced
1 small red onion, chopped
1 red capsicum, chopped
1 jalapeno chilli, seeded
1 tablespoon grated fresh ginger
finely grated rind of 1 lime
1 tablespoon lime juice
1/2 cup (15 g/1/2 oz) coriander
    leaves, chopped

1 Put the diced pineapple, roughly chopped onion, capsicum, chilli and ginger in a food processor and mix, using the pulse button, until coarsely chopped. Stir in the lime rind and juice and the coriander leaves. Season, to taste, with salt and pour into a small bowl.

2 Cover and leave the salsa to stand for 2 hours. Drain off any excess liquid before serving.

NUTRITION PER SERVE
Protein 1 g; Fat 0 g; Carbohydrate 7 g;
Dietary Fibre 2 g; Cholesterol 0 mg;
128 kJ (31 cal)

Cut the skin from the pineapple with a sharp knife.

Cut out the tough eyes from the flesh of the pineapple.

Process the salsa until coarsely chopped then stir in the remaining ingredients.

CUCUMBER AND GINGER SALSA

Shown here with smoked salmon. Also good with chargrilled trout fillet, grilled salmon or tuna, or with cooked prawns.

Preparation time: 10 minutes
+ 15 minutes refrigeration
Total cooking time: Nil
Serves 4

2 Lebanese cucumbers
1 small red onion, finely
    chopped
2 tablespoons chopped pink
    pickled ginger
2 tablespoons chopped mint
1 tablespoon chopped coriander
    leaves
1 tablespoon fish sauce
1 tablespoon lemon juice
3 teaspoons sweet chilli sauce
1 teaspoon sesame oil

1 Peel and cut the cucumbers into cubes and place in a bowl with the onion, ginger, mint and coriander. Mix together well.
2 Add the fish sauce, lemon juice, chilli sauce and sesame oil and toss to combine. Cover and refrigerate for at least 15 minutes before serving.

NUTRITION PER SERVE
Protein 1 g; Fat 1.4 g; Carbohydrate 6 g; Dietary Fibre 1 g; Cholesterol 0 mg; 167 kJ (40 cal)

Pink pickled ginger can be bought at supermarkets and Asian food stores.

Peel the Lebanese cucumbers and cut the flesh into small cubes.

Add the fish sauce, lemon juice, chilli sauce and sesame oil to the salsa.

CHILLI AVOCADO SALSA

Shown here with lamb chops. Also good with corn chips, pitta bread, chargrilled meats and any Mexican food.

Preparation time: 30 minutes
  + 3 hours refrigeration
Total cooking time: Nil
Serves 6

3 tomatoes, seeded and diced
1 small red onion, finely
  chopped
1–2 jalapeno chillies, seeded
  and very finely chopped
1/3 cup (7 g/1/4 oz) flat-leaf
  parsley, chopped
1–2 cloves garlic, crushed
3 tablespoons light olive oil
1 ripe avocado
2 limes, to garnish

1 Mix together the tomato, onion, jalapeno, parsley, garlic and olive oil. Season to taste, cover and refrigerate for 3 hours.
2 Just before serving, halve the avocado, remove the stone and gently mash the flesh with a fork while it is still in the skin. Scoop out the mashed avocado and stir into the salsa. Serve with lime wedges.

NUTRITION PER SERVE
Protein 2 g; Fat 15 g; Carbohydrate 3 g;
Dietary Fibre 2 g; Cholesterol 0 mg;
628 kJ (150 cal)

Cut the tomatoes in half, remove the seeds with a spoon and dice the flesh.

Mix together the tomato, onion, chilli, parsley, garlic and olive oil.

Don't bother to dirty another bowl—it is easier to mash the avocado in its skin.

PAWPAW, PINEAPPLE AND PEANUT SALSA

Shown here with pan-fried fish fillets. Good with any grilled or pan-fried fish or chicken.

Preparation time: 40 minutes
  + standing
Total cooking time: Nil
Serves 6

250 g (8 oz) pawpaw
1/2 small pineapple (about 200 g/ 6½ oz)
1 kiwi fruit
3 spring onions, finely chopped
1 birds-eye chilli, finely sliced
1 tablespoon shredded mint leaves
1 tablespoon lemon juice
1/3 cup (50 g/1¾ oz) honey roasted peanuts, finely chopped

1 Peel the pawpaw, pineapple and kiwi fruit. Remove and discard the seeds from the pawpaw and cut out the hard core of the pineapple.
2 Dice the fruit and combine with the spring onion, chilli, mint, lemon juice and peanuts and season well with black pepper. Cover and leave to stand for a while before serving.

NUTRITION PER SERVE
Protein 1 g; Fat 14 g; Carbohydrate 7 g; Dietary Fibre 2 g; Cholesterol 0 mg; 889 kJ (217 cal)

COOK'S FILE

Note: Choose pawpaw, pineapple and kiwi fruit that are ready to eat, not under- or overripe.

Peel the pawpaw using an ordinary potato peeler.

Peel the fruit, discarding the seeds, and chop the flesh into small cubes.

Mix together all the ingredients, cover and leave to stand for a few minutes.

MANGO, RAISIN AND FRESH TOMATO SALSA

Shown here with sliced beef fillet. Also good with lamb, chicken, fish and seafood.

Preparation time: 40 minutes
Total cooking time: Nil
Serves 4

2 tomatoes
1 mango
50 g (1¾ oz) raisins
1 teaspoon canned green peppercorns, drained and crushed
1 teaspoon finely grated lemon rind
2 tablespoons red wine vinegar
1 tablespoon olive oil
1 spring onion, shredded

1 Score a cross in the base of each tomato. Place in a bowl of boiling water for 10 seconds, then plunge into cold water and peel the skin away from the cross. Scoop out the seeds and discard. Finely chop the flesh.
2 Peel and finely dice the mango and mix with the tomato and raisins. Mix together the peppercorns, lemon rind, vinegar and oil and add to the salsa. Season well and scatter with the spring onion to serve.

NUTRITION PER SERVE
Protein 2 g; Fat 5 g; Carbohydrate 21 g; Dietary Fibre 3 g; Cholesterol 0 mg; 576 kJ (138 cal)

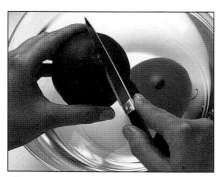

Score a cross in the base of each tomato to make it easier to peel off the skin.

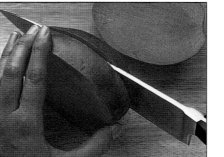

Cut the cheeks from the mango, remove the skin and dice the flesh.

Mix the peppercorns, rind, vinegar and oil with the rest of the salsa ingredients.

Use rubber gloves when slicing chillies, to prevent skin irritation.

Cut the tomatoes in half lengthways and drizzle with the oil.

Simmer the beans for 40 minutes, or until they are tender.

Mix together all the salsa ingredients until they are well combined.

BEAN AND CHILLI SALSA

Shown here with chargrilled tuna, but also good with chargrilled chicken, lamb or beef.

Preparation time: 20 minutes
 + 12 hours soaking
Total cooking time: 2 hours 45 minutes
Serves 8

³/4 **cup (150 g/5 oz) dried pinto
  beans**
8 Roma tomatoes
1 tablespoon olive oil
**3 red chillies, seeded and thinly
  sliced**
2 cloves garlic, finely chopped
3 tablespoons lime juice
**¹/2 cup (15 g/¹/2 oz) coriander
  leaves, finely chopped**

1 Soak the beans in cold water for 12 hours or overnight.
2 Preheat the oven to moderate 180°C (350°F/Gas 4). Cut the tomatoes in half lengthways and place in a shallow baking dish. Drizzle with the oil and season well with salt and pepper. Cook for 2 hours, then cool slightly and cut into small pieces.
3 Drain and rinse the beans. Place in a large pan and cover with cold water. Bring to the boil and simmer for 40 minutes, or until tender. Drain and rinse well. Leave to cool.
4 Place the beans, tomato, chilli, garlic, lime juice and coriander in a bowl and mix until well combined.

NUTRITION PER SERVE
Protein 5 g; Fat 3 g; Carbohydrate 11 g; Dietary Fibre 4 g; Cholesterol 0 mg; 311 kJ (74 cal)

EGGPLANT, CAPSICUM AND OLIVE SALSA

Shown here with Italian woodfired bread. Also good with grilled or barbecued beef, lamb or chicken.

Preparation time: 45 minutes + cooling
Total cooking time: 20 minutes
Serves 6

1 medium eggplant, diced
2 tablespoons olive oil
1/2 teaspoon salt
1 large red capsicum, diced
12 Kalamata olives, pitted and
    finely chopped
4 spring onions, finely chopped
1 small red chilli, chopped
2 cloves garlic, crushed
1 tablespoon olive oil
2 teaspoons red wine vinegar
2 teaspoons lemon juice
1 tablespoon chopped parsley
2 teaspoons chopped chives

1 Preheat the oven to moderate 180°C (350°F/Gas 4). Toss the eggplant with the olive oil and the salt, then place in a single layer on a baking tray. Cook for about 20 minutes, or until golden and cooked. Remove from the oven and allow to cool.

2 Gently mix the eggplant with the capsicum, olives, spring onion, chilli, garlic, olive oil, vinegar, lemon juice and salt and freshly ground black pepper, to taste.

3 Stir through the parsley and chives and serve at room temperature.

NUTRITION PER SERVE
Protein 2 g; Fat 10 g; Carbohydrate 4 g; Dietary Fibre 3 g; Cholesterol 0 mg; 472 kJ (113 cal)

COOK'S FILE

Note: Make sure the eggplant does not have large hard or dark seeds—these are unpalatable and will make the salsa bitter. If you find them, cut them out before roasting the eggplant.

If you are very fond of olives, invest in an olive pitter to make the task simple.

Toss the eggplant with the olive oil and salt before roasting.

Add salt and pepper to the mixture, to your taste.

Stir through the parsley and chives and serve at room temperature.

TOMATO SALSA

Shown here with pan-fried veal. Also good with chicken, seafood, grilled meats and Mexican food.

Preparation time: 30 minutes
+ 1 hour refrigeration
Total cooking time: Nil
Serves 6

4 Roma tomatoes
1 red onion
1 birds eye chilli
3 tablespoons chopped
coriander leaves
1–2 tablespoons lime juice
1/2 teaspoon salt

1 Cut the tomatoes in half horizontally and scoop out the seeds with a teaspoon. Finely chop the tomato flesh and the onion.
2 Wearing plastic gloves, cut the chilli in half. Remove the membrane and seeds and finely slice the flesh.
3 Mix together all the ingredients, cover and refrigerate for 1 hour.

NUTRITION PER SERVE
Protein 1 g; Fat 0 g; Carbohydrate 2 g; Dietary Fibre 1 g; Cholesterol 0 mg; 52 kJ (13 cal)

Cut the tomatoes in half lengthways and scoop out the seeds with a teaspoon.

Finely chop the onion into small uniform pieces, using a sharp knife.

Limes produce a varying amount of juice, depending on the season.

PEAR, CORIANDER AND ONION SALSA

Shown here with pan-fried butterfly pork steak. Also good with beef, chicken or duck.

Preparation time: 35 minutes
Total cooking time: Nil
Serves 8

3 beurre bosc pears
3–4 tablespoons lime juice
1 red onion, finely diced
3/4 cup (25 g/3/4 oz) coriander
  leaves, finely chopped
1/2 teaspoon chilli flakes
1 teaspoon finely grated lime
  rind

1 Cut the pears into quarters, remove the cores and chop into small dice. Sprinkle with the lime juice.
2 Combine the pear, onion, coriander, chilli flakes and lime rind and season with salt and pepper, to taste.

NUTRITION PER SERVE
Protein 1 g; Fat 0 g; Carbohydrate 17 g;
Dietary Fibre 3 g; Cholesterol 0 mg;
290 kJ (69 cal)

COOK'S FILE

Note: Use pears that are just ready to eat, not overripe and floury fruit.

To dice an onion, slice it almost to the root, two or three times.

Then slice through vertically, leaving the root to hold it together. Then chop finely.

Cut the pears into quarters, then remove the cores and chop into dice.

Cut the capsicum into quarters and remove the seeds and membrane.

Cut the tomatoes in half, scoop out the seeds and cut the flesh into strips.

Peel the limes, then cut away the pith and cut the flesh into segments.

Mix together all the ingredients and leave to stand, for the flavours to develop.

ROASTED RED CAPSICUM, TOMATO, LIME AND CHILLI SALSA

Shown here with chargrilled lamb steaks. Also good with veal, meat, chicken, fish and seafood.

Preparation time: 45 minutes
Total cooking time: 35 minutes
Serves 6

**2 red capsicums
2 tomatoes
1/2 small red onion
1–2 small red chillies
2 limes
2 tablespoons olive oil
1 teaspoon sugar**

1 Preheat the oven to moderate 180°C (350°F/Gas 4). Cut the capsicums into quarters and discard the membrane and seeds. Place in an oiled baking dish and bake for 30 minutes, turning regularly. If the capsicum begins to burn, add 2 tablespoons of water to the baking dish. Allow to cool and then chop into small cubes.
2 Score a cross in the base of each tomato. Place in a bowl of boiling water for 10 seconds, then plunge into cold water and peel the skin away from the cross. Cut the tomatoes in half and scoop out the seeds with a teaspoon. Cut the tomato flesh into thin strips.
3 Finely chop the onion and chilli. Peel the limes, then cut off the pith and carefully cut the flesh into fine segments.
4 Mix together the capsicum, tomato, onion, chilli, lime segments, olive oil and sugar in a bowl. Season well with salt and freshly ground black pepper. Cover and leave to stand for at least 15 minutes for the flavours to blend, before serving.

NUTRITION PER SERVE
Protein 2 g; Fat 7 g; Carbohydrate 4 g; Dietary Fibre 2 g; Cholesterol 0 mg; 348 kJ (83 cal)

ROASTED CORN, AVOCADO AND GREEN OLIVE SALSA

Shown here with pan-fried salmon. Also good with chicken, lamb and beef.

Preparation time: 35 minutes
 + 15 minutes refrigeration
Total cooking time: 20 minutes
Serves 6

2 corn cobs, husks removed
1 avocado
90 g (3 oz) stuffed green olives, chopped
2 tablespoons finely chopped parsley
3 spring onions, shredded
1 tablespoon olive oil
2 tablespoons lemon juice

1 Cook the corn cobs in a pan of boiling water for 5 minutes, or until just soft. Drain, cool and pat dry with paper towels. Using a large sharp knife, cut the kernels from the cob and place in a single layer on a foil-lined grill tray. Grill under a very hot grill for 10 minutes, or until the corn is golden brown, turning the kernels once during grilling to ensure even roasting. Allow to cool.
2 Remove the avocado stone and peel. Chop the flesh into small pieces.
3 Combine the corn, avocado, olives, parsley, spring onion, olive oil and lemon juice, and season liberally with salt and freshly ground black pepper. Toss well to make sure the avocado is coated with dressing. Cover and chill for 15 minutes before serving.

NUTRITION PER SERVE
Protein 2 g; Fat 20 g; Carbohydrate 7 g; Dietary Fibre 3 g; Cholesterol 0 mg; 900 kJ (215 cal)

COOK'S FILE

Variation: Green olives are an acquired taste. You could use a small green capsicum cut into thin strips.

Remove the husks from the corn cobs and cook in boiling water.

Grill the corn kernels until golden brown, turning once during cooking.

Remove the stone and peel from the avocado and cut the flesh into cubes.

Mix together all the salsa ingredients, seasoning well with salt and pepper.

PAPAYA AND BLACK BEAN SALSA

Shown here with chargrilled blue-eyed cod cutlets. Also good with salmon or tuna steaks, chicken, beef and lamb.

Preparation time: 25 minutes
Total cooking time: Nil
Serves 4

1 small red onion, finely chopped
1 papaya (about 500 g/1 lb), peeled, seeded and cubed
1 birds eye chilli, seeded and finely chopped
1 tablespoon salted black beans, rinsed and drained
2 teaspoons peanut oil
1 teaspoon sesame oil
2 teaspoons fish sauce
1 tablespoon lime juice
1 tablespoon chopped coriander leaves
2 teaspoons shredded mint

1 In a bowl, gently toss together the onion, papaya, chilli and black beans with your hands.
2 Just before serving, whisk together the peanut oil, sesame oil, fish sauce and lime juice. Pour over the salsa and gently toss. Add the coriander and mint and serve immediately, at room temperature.

NUTRITION PER SERVE
Protein 1 g; Fat 4 g; Carbohydrate 5 g; Dietary Fibre 1 g; Cholesterol 0 mg; 224 kJ (53 cal)

COOK'S FILE

Note: Black beans have a distinctive taste, so if you are not familiar with them, taste them before adding to the salsa. If you prefer not to add them, the salsa is equally delicious without.
Variation: Pawpaw can be used instead of papaya. It is a larger fruit from the same family, with yellower flesh and a less sweet flavour.

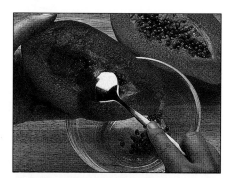

Cut the papaya in half and scoop out the seeds with a spoon.

The best way to toss the salsa, without breaking up the fruit, is with your hands.

Whisk together the oil dressing and add the salsa just before serving.

Serving chart

The following is an easy-to-read chart showing which sauces and salsas are traditionally served with which foods. This, of course, is simply a guide... there might be people who secretly eat their pasta with gravy, their Christmas pudding with butterscotch sauce, or their toast with pineapple salsa, but these are our suggestions.

Sauces

BEEF	PAN-FRIED, GRILLED OR BARBECUED STEAK	Green peppercorn ■ Tomato pasta ■ Demi-glace ■ Leek and pine nut ■ Creamy mushroom ■ Gravy ■ Pawpaw ■ Bearnaise ■ Black bean ■ Spicy roasted pumpkin and red capsicum ■ Rocket salsa verde ■ Tomato and red chilli ■ Roasted cashew satay ■ Barbecue ■ Skordalia ■ Almond and red capsicum ■ Roasted red capsicum ■ Japanese soy, mirin and sesame ■ Chunky roasted red onion
	ROAST	Gravy ■ Bearnaise ■ Tomato and red chilli
	CORNED BEEF	Classic white (béchamel)
	COLD MEATS	Cumberland ■ Sour cherry ■ Champagne apple
	SAUSAGES	Barbecue ■ Roasted cashew satay ■ Roasted red capsicum
	HAMBURGERS	Barbecue ■ Roasted cashew satay ■ Roasted red capsicum
LAMB	PAN-FRIED, GRILLED CHOPS OR FILLETS	Pawpaw ■ Spiced coconut ■ Black bean ■ Almond and red capsicum ■ Spicy pumpkin and red capsicum ■ Leek and pine nut ■ Skordalia ■ Sweet and sour ■ Roasted red onion ■ Roasted red capsicum ■ Tomato and red chilli
	ROAST	Gravy ■ Mint
PORK	PAN-FRIED, GRILLED OR BARBECUED	Sweet and sour ■ Apple ■ Pawpaw ■ Black bean ■ Champagne apple ■ Roasted cashew satay
	ROAST	Cranberry ■ Apple ■ Gravy ■ Sour cherry ■ Champagne apple
	HAM	Cumberland ■ Sour cherry ■ Champagne apple
VEAL	PAN-FRIED	Velouté ■ Tomato pasta ■ Creamy mushroom ■ Leek and pine nut ■ Chunky roasted red onion ■ Tomato and chilli ■ Roasted red capsicum
GAME		Sour Cherry ■ Gravy
PASTA		Bolognese ■ Tomato pasta ■ Pesto ■ Almond and red capsicum ■ Roasted walnut ■ Leek and pine nut ■ Rocket salsa verde

CHICKEN /TURKEY	PAN-FRIED, BARBECUED OR GRILLED	Green peppercorn ∎ Cumberland ∎ Satay ∎ Hollandaise ∎ Skordalia ∎ Creamy mushroom ∎ Mint and yoghurt ∎ Champagne apple ∎ Almond and red capsicum ∎ Leek and pine nut ∎ Rocket salsa verde ∎ Tomato and red chilli ∎ Black bean ∎ Sour cherry ∎ Chinese lemon ∎ Bombay lime ∎ Velouté ∎ Roasted cashew satay ∎ Pawpaw ∎ Pesto ∎ Roasted red capsicum
	ROAST	Cranberry ∎ Gravy ∎ Bread

SEAFOOD

SHELLFISH	PRAWNS, LOBSTER, CRAB	Skordalia ∎ Blue cheese, pecan and cognac grilling sauce ∎ Cheese (mornay) ∎ Bombay lime
	OYSTERS, MUSSELS	Almond and red capsicum ∎ Black bean ∎ Cheese (mornay) ∎ Velouté
	SCALLOPS	Japanese soy, mirin and sesame ∎ Velouté ∎ Beurre blanc ∎ Bombay lime
SALMON	PAN-FRIED STEAKS	Sweet and sour ∎ Satay ∎ Beurre blanc
	POACHED WHOLE OR FILLETS	Hollandaise ∎ Sorrel and lemon ∎ Bearnaise ∎ Bombay lime ∎ Leek and pine nut
TUNA	PAN-FRIED OR BARBECUED STEAKS	Almond and red capsicum ∎ Spicy roasted pumpkin and red capsicum ∎ Chilli spiced mango ∎ Bombay lime ∎ Beurre blanc
WHITE FILLETS	PAN-FRIED, GRILLED, BARBECUED OR DEEP-FRIED	Satay ∎ Rocket salsa verde ∎ Sweet and sour ∎ Satay ∎ Gazpacho ∎ Pesto ∎ Spiced Coconut ∎ Bombay lime ∎ Velouté ∎ Beurre blanc
WHOLE FISH	BAKED, PAN-FRIED OR BARBECUED	Chilli spiced mango ∎ Tomato and red chilli ∎ Sorrel and lemon ∎ Chinese lemon ∎ Veloute ∎ Classic white (béchamel) ∎ Cheese (mornay)

VEGETABLES	ARTICHOKES	Beurre blanc ∎ Bombay lime
	ASPARAGUS	Hollandaise ∎ Gazpacho ∎ Beurre blanc ∎ Bombay lime
	EGGPLANT	Skordalia
	BROCCOLI	Classic white (béchamel)
	CAULIFLOWER	Classic white (béchamel)
	POTATOES	Gravy ∎ Leek and pine nut ∎ Spicy roasted pumpkin and red capsicum
	TOMATOES	Pesto
	GRILLED, STEAMED OR BOILED VEGETABLES	Roasted red capsicum ∎ Japanese soy, mirin and sesame ∎ Beurre blanc ∎ Roasted walnut Hollandaise ∎ Japanese soy, mirin and sesame ∎ Cheese (mornay) ∎ Spiced coconut ∎ Tomato and red chilli ∎ Chinese lemon ∎ Beurre blanc ∎ Skordalia
	AVOCADO	Blue cheese, pecan and cognac grilling sauce

DESSERTS		
FRESH FRUIT	Iced orange ▪ Burnt sugar ▪ Praline cream ▪ Brandy cream ▪ Chocolate rum ▪ Berry coulis
POACHED FRUIT	Zabaglione ▪ Burnt sugar ▪ Coconut lime anglaise ▪ Praline cream ▪ Hot chocolate ▪ Brandy cream ▪ Butterscotch ▪ Berry coulis
ICE CREAM	Burnt sugar ▪ Chocolate rum ▪ Berry coulis
PANCAKES/WAFFLES	Iced orange ▪ Burnt sugar ▪ Praline cream ▪ Hot chocolate ▪ Butterscotch ▪ Chocolate rum
STEAMED PUDDINGS	Vanilla custard ▪ Coconut lime anglaise ▪ Hot chocolate ▪ Brandy cream ▪ Butterscotch ▪ Chocolate rum
FRUIT PIES AND TARTS	Vanilla custard ▪ Coconut lime anglaise ▪ Brandy cream ▪ Berry coulis ▪ Crème anglaise

Salsas

BEEF
Chargrilled vegetable ▪ Pumpkin seed ▪ Bocconcini, tomato and sun-dried capsicum ▪ Chilli avocado ▪ Eggplant, capsicum and olive ▪ Mango, raisin and fresh tomato ▪ Bean and chilli ▪ Tomato ▪ Peach, red capsicum and ginger ▪ Roasted red capsicum, tomato, lime and chilli ▪ Pear, coriander and onion ▪ Roasted corn, avocado and green olive ▪ Papaya and black bean

LAMB
Chilli avocado ▪ Chargrilled vegetable ▪ Pumpkin seed ▪ Bocconcini, tomato and sun-dried capsicum ▪ Mango, raisin and fresh tomato ▪ Bean and chilli ▪ Eggplant, capsicum and olive ▪ Tomato ▪ Pear, coriander and onion ▪ Roasted red capsicum, tomato, lime and chilli ▪ Papaya and black bean ▪ Roasted corn, avocado and green olive

PORK
Chargrilled vegetable ▪ Pumpkin seed ▪ Bocconcini, tomato and sun-dried capsicum ▪ Melon ▪ Chilli avocado ▪ Tomato ▪ Pear, coriander and onion ▪ Roasted red capsicum, tomato, lime and chilli

VEAL
Chargrilled vegetable ▪ Pumpkin seed ▪ Chilli avocado ▪ Melon ▪ Peach, red capsicum and ginger ▪ Tomato ▪ Roasted red capsicum, tomato lime and chilli

CHICKEN
Chargrilled vegetable ▪ Pumpkin seed ▪ Bocconcini, tomato and sun-dried capsicum ▪ Pineapple ▪ Pawpaw, pineapple and peanut ▪ Mango, raisin and fresh tomato ▪ Bean and chilli ▪ Tomato ▪ Eggplant, capsicum and olive ▪ Papaya and black bean ▪ Melon ▪ Peach, red capsicum and ginger ▪ Roasted red capsicum, tomato, lime and chilli ▪ Roasted corn, avocado and green olive ▪ Pear, coriander and onion

DUCK
Pear, coriander and onion

FISH
Bocconcini, tomato and sun-dried capsicum ▪ Pineapple ▪ Pawpaw, pineapple and peanut ▪ Cucumber and ginger ▪ Bean and chilli ▪ Tomato ▪ Peach, red capsicum and ginger ▪ Mango, raisin and fresh tomato ▪ Roasted red capsicum, tomato, lime and chilli ▪ Melon ▪ Roasted corn, avocado and green olive ▪ Papaya and black bean

SHELLFISH
Cucumber and ginger ▪ Bocconcini, tomato and sun-dried capsicum ▪ Peach, red capsicum and ginger ▪ Mango, raisin and fresh tomato ▪ Tomato ▪ Roasted red capsicum, tomato, lime and chilli ▪ Melon

INDEX

INTERNATIONAL GLOSSARY OF INGREDIENTS

baby squash	pattypan squash	cornflour	cornstarch	mince	ground meat
bicarbonate of soda	baking soda	cream	single/light	plain flour	all-purpose flour
bok choy	pak choi		whipping cream	prawn	shrimp
broad beans	fava beans	dark chocolate	plain chocolate	rocket	arugula
butternut	squash	eggplant	aubergine	Roma tomato	egg/plum tomato
pumpkin		flat-leaf parsley	Italian parsley	snow pea	mangetout
capsicum	pepper	golden syrup	use dark corn	soft brown sugar	light brown sugar
caster sugar	superfine sugar		syrup	spring onion	scallion
chick peas	garbanzo beans	ground almonds	almond meal	tomato paste	passata/sieved
chilli	chile, chili pepper	icing sugar	confectioners' sugar	(Aus./US)	crushed
coriander	cilantro	Lebanese cucumber	short cucumber		tomatoes (UK)

This edition published in 2003 by Bay Books, an imprint of Murdoch Magazines Pty Limited,
GPO Box 1203, Sydney NSW 2001, Australia.

Managing Editor: Rachel Carter. **Editors:** Elizabeth Cotton, Jane Price **Designer:** Wing Ping Tong **Food Director:** Jody Vassallo. **Food Editor:** Roslyn Anderson **Recipe Development:** Roslyn Anderson, Amanda Cooper, Alex Diblasi, Michelle Earl, Jo Glynn, Barbara Lowery, Sally Parker, Jo Richardson, Alison Turner **Home Economists:** Michelle Lawton, Toiva Longhurst, Kerrie Mullins, Angela Nahas, Justine Poole, Kerrie Ray **Photographers:** Tony Lyon, George Mourtzakis, Reg Morrison (steps) **Food Stylist:** Kay Francis **Food Stylist (special features):** Roslyn Anderson **Food Preparation:** Liz Nolan
Chief Executive: Juliet Rogers. **Publisher:** Kay Scarlett.

The nutritional information provided for each recipe does not include any accompaniments, such as rice, unless they are listed in the ingredients. The values are approximations and can be affected by biological and seasonal variations in food, the unknown composition of some manufactured foods and uncertainty in the dietary database. Nutrient data given are derived primarily from the NUTTAB95 database produced by the Australian New Zealand Food Authority.

ISBN 0 86411 700 0.
Reprinted 2004. Printed by Sing Cheong Printing Co. Ltd. PRINTED IN CHINA.